Positioned To Be Found

How To Prepare Yourself For Marriage **Right Now**

TERESA RENEE HUNT

Truth2RenewHearts Enterprises, LLC

POSITIONED TO BE FOUND

Published by Truth2RenewHearts Enterprises, LLC

ISBN-13: 978-0986448201
ISBN-10: 0986448206

Cover design by Soleil Meade, Soleil Branding Essentials
Professional Book Editing Services by Dr. LaShonda Fuller, Truth UnTold Enterprises, LLC

Unless other indicated, Scripture quotations are from:
The Holy Bible, New International Version

The examples used in this book are compilations of stories from real situations. But names, facts, and issues have been altered to protect confidentiality while illustrating the points. The ideas, suggestions, general principles and conclusions presented here reflect the view of the author and your implementation of the information provided should be adapted to fit your own particular situation or circumstance. The author/publisher has made every effort to ensure the accuracy of the information herein. However, the information contained in this book is provided without warranty, either express or implied.

For information:
TRUTH2RENEWHEARTS ENTERPRISES, LLC
Info@teresareneehunt.com

For booking information:
Truth2RenewHearts Enterprises, LLC
Booking@teresareneehunt.com

DEDICATION

To my husband Julian for 'finding me'! I love you! I thank God that I was found by such a wonderful man. You are truly a gift to me. I consider it a blessing that I am able to spend my life with you!

To singles everywhere, including the sisters in the Ready4TheRing Movement who are ready to position themselves to receive God's best for their lives and not only have the desire to be married, but will align their desires with their decision making; Be strong and steadfast in the Lord. Do not get weary in well doing. Keep the faith!

To women who have experienced sexual assault; with the prayer that you will allow God to heal you emotionally, physically, spiritually, and mentally! Know that He is able to do this and more!

INTRODUCTION

Do you dream about your **wedding day** and becoming a **wife** soon?

Are you curious about what men ***really*** want and what it takes to be found by a good one?

Are you **tired** of attracting the wrong men, sick of being alone, and broken after you have given your all?

Are you **ready** to experience more happiness and fulfillment in your life and relationships?

Do you want to know the ***secret*** to relationship success and becoming a wife?

PERFECT! I am thrilled that you have a copy of this book in your hands!

Inside this book you will discover:

- ✓ How to attract your "Boaz" and become his wife.
- ✓ Exactly what is keeping you "stuck" and has held you back from experiencing true love & a long-lasting relationship.

- ✓ How to date in a way which is healthy, enjoyable, and leads to a marital covenant.

- ✓ How to recognize a good man and be able to distinguish whether he views you as Mrs. Right, or Ms. Right Now.

- ✓ The top 13 ways to position yourself to be found and prepare yourself to be a wife.

- ✓ And SO much more!

I wrote this book just for you! To help you develop healthy dating habits, avoid dead-end relationships, and experience true love & fulfillment. I wrote this book to share with you what it takes to stand out as a "good thing" to a man who is looking for a wife!

I'm sharing with you proven relationship wisdom that will help you avoid common pitfalls and mistakes. Since I know now the importance of aligning your decisions while single, with your desire to be a wife one day, I do not want to keep all the juicy details and RelationTips to myself! I want to help you date wisely, and position you to become an even better woman, so you can be a better wife in the future.

I wrote this book to help you get **#Ready4TheRing**!

I am so excited to guide you on your journey to preparing yourself for marriage, becoming a wife, and experiencing the life and love you truly desire!

As you are about to dive into the book, let me tell you what to expect. Each chapter begins with a "**Jewel of Wisdom**", a short message relevant to the chapter title, and the life-transformational content inside! In each chapter you will encounter very real and relevant topics that all women can relate to! Expect to be challenged. Expect to be encouraged. Expect to be transformed as you read this book. At the end of each chapter, I share a "Ready4TheRing Plan of Action". Consider this section a time of reflection, renewal, support, and preparation with me as your coach. You may even want to read the book more than once so you can get the full book experience and miss nothing!

I would love to hear from you while you are reading! I welcome you to share your AHA moments with me on social media using the hashtag **#positionedtobefound**.

Let's connect now before you start reading. My social media info is listed below. I also invite you to take a quick picture "selfie" with the book!

Share with the world that you have your copy and that you are preparing yourself for marriage right now!

Let's Connect!

Facebook: @Ready 4 The Ring with Teresa R. Hunt

Twitter: @teresareneehunt

Instagram: @Ready4thering

LinkedIn: @ Teresa Renee Hunt

Alright, I certainly don't want to keep you from diving in to get all the Jewels of Wisdom and RelationTips! It is time to get you Ready4TheRing!

Now on to Chapter One!

With Hugs,

Teresa Renee

CONTENTS

Part 1: Be Real – Take Off The Mask

Part 2: Align Your Decisions With Your Desires

Part 3: Prepare And Position Yourself

Chapter 1: **Break The Silence: Be Healed, Be Free, Be Whole**

❖ *Jewel of Wisdom:*

Preparing your heart for love includes the process of healing and becoming whole. You must choose healing over neglecting, ignoring, or numbing the pain of your past and present. Be healed. Be Free. Be whole. Going through the healing process will free you of emotional-baggage and more importantly, increase your ability to give and receive true love. #Ready4TheRing

As a Christian woman, a leader in the church, someone who women of all ages have looked up to, I secretly believed that I always needed to "have it all together". Being raised with a strict upbringing and Christian values - I thought I needed to maintain a certain image in order to keep everyone proud. These are just *some* of the reasons why I allowed myself to "*hide my pain*".

I would have never said it like this before, but honestly, I was wearing a mask. I had not intended to live this way, however my smile, makeup, wardrobe, and polite manners, kept others from suspecting that I would ever be dealing with such brokenness internally. No one would have known I was hurting inside, and I convinced myself that I would be just fine. Plus, who could I talk to and *really* be honest with?

Can you relate? I bet you can! Many of us hesitate to share what we struggle with daily, for fear of judgment and lack of trust in others with our personal lives.

Just like you, for years, I carried a suitcase full of baggage.

February 27, 2001 was a life altering day, one that I will never forget. It was the day that left me emotionally broken and empty, vulnerable, mentally bruised, and spiritually numb.

It was on that day that I mastered the art of a chameleon; I became very skilled at wearing a mask. I became one who was excellent at pretending, forgetting, and covering up. I would not have named my once guiltless-strengths as such back then, but as I am completely honest with myself and you, I have realized the effects that entire day had on me, and the description above would explain it.

I vividly remember the day.

I stood at the bus stop trying to process how I was going to tell my parents, or if I even *should.* I was a junior in high school and at the point failing math. It was a requirement that my family and I discuss the tutoring options available within the college preparation program I was privileged to attend so I could pass my math course.

I rode in silence that day as I sat on the Port Authority bus to meet my parents and the director of the program. My mind was racing. How was I going to sit in the meeting after what just happened? The truth was, I really wanted to cry as the bus crept along to my stop. Deep inside I was screaming, I was angry, violated, and I wanted to weep and release all of my anguish, despair, and shame. If it is true that tears bring healing and renewal, at that very moment, I wish I would have cried a river. But I didn't. I buried my hurt and pain. As the bus approached my destination, I gave myself a pep-talk, and walked off the bus with a fixed disposition. I knew I would have to pretend as if nothing ever happened. With my best attempt, I tried to put on a "good face" so no one in the meeting would know I had just been raped.

Going from being sexually violated to walking into a meeting to sit face-to-face with my parents, left me little time to process what just actually happened. Instead of dealing with the suffering of being raped, I pushed it out of my mind and proceeded with what I thought would be my normal life; however I did not know that life for me would be much different.

As I sat in the meeting, feeling hopeless because not only were my grades suffering, but now my already distorted self-image suffered even more, I felt overwhelmed. After failed attempts of holding back the tears, like pouring rain being released from dark gray clouds, the storm began to roll down my face. The paranoia of whether or not my parents would notice something was different about me ate away at my conscience like termites on an old wooden post. I was too afraid to share what happened, because at that moment in time, I believed the appalling lie that I "the victim" was to blame. Therefore, I sat in the conference with snuffles and tears streaming down my face, which was actually fitting for me as a failing high school student with parents who expected nothing less than academic success from their only child. Later that night, I tried my best to erase the memory of what happened from my mind by pretending it did not happen, as I figured this would be the best thing to do. After all, I would have to face him, my perpetrator, in class the next day.

He eyed me as I walked into class, smiled, flirted, and said that he would call me later that night, and he did. He called that day, the next, and continued for many days after. He wanted to spend time with me, he wanted to have sex. He paid more attention to me than he ever did. Although he continued to pursue me, I did not accept his offer. I did not want him to take anything else from me, as he had already stolen my virginity.

At the age of 16, he robbed me of my innocence, and just like many thefts after breaking into a victim's space, he too left indication of his violation. In my case, he left a once pure teenage girl with emotional confusion, twisted ideals of sex, misconceptions about relationships, mental scars, and emotional baggage. He also left me with a distorted interpretation of what it meant to be liked and admired by a guy. With all of the attention he gave me, even after non-consensual sex, I became deceived into believing a mistruth that women, who willingly connect their bodies with a man, accept as true: "Sex keeps a man attracted and attached to you; and men express their admiration for you through sex".

Sifting through the overwhelming emotions of the day was too much to handle. Moreover, I felt obliged to remain silent. After all, rape victims are very rarely believed. Plus, this guy was popular and he was an upperclassman. I did not want to be humiliated, blamed, interrogated, or isolated. I had already blamed myself, and that was enough. I was in need of healing and counsel, but I was so ashamed and afraid, I didn't know where to turn.

Because I was a Christian, and I knew the Word of God, which says to forgive, that is what I did. He never apologized or acknowledged what he did, but I forgave him. I blocked the incident out of my mind and never looked back. Actually, I thought forgiveness *was* my healing. It was not until over 10 years later when I realized forgiveness only initiated the healing process but did not make the process complete. Just a few years ago, I realized I took one step into the healing process but never allowed the wound to heal completely. Instead, I kept a band-aid over my internal abrasion and I numbed the pain.

Do you remember the not-so-accurate lesson I believed: that having sex with a man keeps him around, and sex is an expression of admiration? Well, that subconscious belief played out in my dealings with men. Being in relationships and dating was the medicine I used to numb my pain, rebuild myself, and validate my self-image. Men gave me compliments, wanted to spend time with me, bought me gifts, and treated me to nice places. Accepting their attention and gifts caused me not to even think about my secret pain. The more occupied I was, the less I had time to think about or reflect on my emotional brokenness. It was almost as if the offense, heartbreak, and baggage did notexist.

That was until, I was all alone. No friends, no man, no family, just me (and God).

So truthfully, I made it a point *not* to be alone. In a sense, I *needed* to relate to someone on any level. I *needed* to hang with a group of people. I *wanted* to be in relationships because when I was occupied and involved, I felt good about life and about myself.

So as you can tell, I became stuck in a cycle of cover-up relationships and having a “Band-Aid boo”. I was <u>secretly</u> stuck in this cycle from high school through college because I never fully healed. I really never allowed myself the TIME to heal. I knew deep inside, that I was dealing with emotional-baggage I needed to release from my life, but I did not want to deal with the baggage “head on” because I preferred to pretend it didn’t exist. I was avoiding the space I would have to allow God to complete an internal makeover within me. This situation of rape is just one of <u>*many*</u> situations I dealt with that left me brokenhearted and empty. I know I am using very strong and candid language as I describe the sentiments I have experienced, but let me tell you, identifying the TRUTH will FREE you!

ARE *YOU* WEARING A MASK?

Whether you have been hurt by your ex, a family member, your friend, or a church member - we all have encountered some form of emotional, spiritual, or maybe even physical pain. When we experience times like this, typically our reaction is to cover it up, ignore it, or try to get over it on our own. Because we want to maintain our image, and 'put our best foot forward', we hide our pain as we put on our mask of happiness, satisfaction, joy, and fulfillment. We smile in public; we beautify our faces with makeup, eye shadow, blush, and a popping lip color. We leave the house with a high fashion ensemble and a pair of sexy heels. We strut into work, church, bible study, choir rehearsal, prayer meeting, and all the places in between only to return home empty, regretful, brokenhearted, unfulfilled, hurt, and discontented. That's right - we look good from head to toe, we are dressed-to-kill, but the pain and emotional-baggage is *killing us* inside.

THE IRONY OF THE MASK

Did you see the places I named above? Isn't it unbelievable that we actually go to church, bible study, choir rehearsal, prayer meeting, and more, yet still carry so much baggage and hurt? We go into the house of God several times throughout each week, yet we do not allow the God of the house into OUR temple. We don't completely allow Him into our heart or mind so that he can bring healing to our soul. How do I know this? I know because I have been there, and I personally know many women who *still* live this way. Are you one of them?

Inside we believe it is easier to ignore, overlook, or discount the fact that we are hurting emotionally. It is this trick of the enemy that causes us to become so accustomed to living with the pain that we believe our condition is truly a part of our life we cannot change. We justify the idea that we must live with the pain because "it is what it is". Other times we become so accustomed to carrying the hurt that we are numb and don't even recognize that the very thing we have not confronted, has now been in control of our lives, always confronting us.

BREAK THE SILENCE!

I did not know the exact cycle that I was trapped in with a "Band-Aid boo" and wearing a mask while I was in bondage, but I know now. I am only able to recognize this truth now because I AM healed. Once I began to desire a CHANGE in my life, I realized I had to be honest and allow God to renew and heal my mind, heart, emotions, and spirit. Once I opened myself up for God to work on me, I also became aware that the effects of this one situation and many others had power over my life and nearly governed every decision I made relative to men and relationships thereafter.

As I look back over my life, I have realized:

"*You can choose healing, or you can neglect the process and try to overlook and numb the pain. Being healed will free you, whereas choosing not to directly address the hurts will cause you to be held hostage by your own emotional baggage.*"

Hiding the fact that I had been raped, being silent about the incident and my pain, and also trying to get over it *on my own* actually allowed my hurt to perpetuate. Note this: **Secrets Breed In Silence** *and* **Pain Grows In Silence.**

This is why it is extremely important to break the silence about your hurt. Take off the mask and reveal your pain in order to BE HEALED. You will find that the root of many of your habits, especially while relating to men will be linked to that very thing. Did you know that many of the habits we display, and choices we make while dating are in direct correlation to past experiences which include past hurts? *Your* pain may not have been caused by rape, but now is the time to identify and be honest about what *has* hurt you. Maybe you have been cheated on, neglected, deceived, abused, heartbroken, emotionally mislead, hurt by the church, a family member, and more!

NOW is the time to **BREAK THE SILENCE** on your brokenness.

BREAK THE SILENCE about your loneliness.

BREAK THE SILENCE about your emptiness.

BREAK THE SILENCE about the domestic violence you endured.

BREAK THE SILENCE about your un-forgiveness.

BREAK THE SILENCE about your emotional pain.

BREAK THE SILENCE about what caused your low self-esteem.

BREAK THE SILENCE about your abortion.

BREAK THE SILENCE about the offense you are carrying.

BREAK THE SILENCE about being raped.

Whatever you are dealing with, whatever the pain may be, whatever secret you are holding onto - it is time to BREAK THE SILENCE!

When I say **BREAK THE SILENCE** I mean that you must ACKNOWLEDGE and IDENTIFY what you are carrying internally that no one can see which has been affecting your life, your ability to be rational, your relationships, and your ability to give and/or receive true love.

When I say **BREAK THE SILENCE**, I mean you must be willing to speak/say/share what happened *to* you and/or the affects that a certain experience has had *on* you. I am not telling you to shout your circumstances, hurt, or baggage from the rooftops. No, I *am* saying, "BE REAL with yourself and BE REAL with GOD." Breaking the silence means that you are no longer going to keep quiet about what you are battling with on the inside. You will no longer worry about what others will think and what they will say. Your main concern will be your healing! You will identify it and have the courage to share this with God instead of keeping it to yourself. The bible says to cast your cares on Him, because He cares for you (1 Peter 5:7). Let me tell you this, God is an omnipotent, all knowing God - so He is already aware of what you are dealing with. However, you activate His ability to move in your life once you acknowledge *to* Him that very thing you are battling.

You see, God does not impose Himself on anyone. You've heard it before that He is a perfect gentleman. God only goes where He is welcomed and moves where He is invited.

When I say it is time to Break the Silence about your hurt, it is because ***God can only heal that which you reveal***.

I share this with you because if you truly want to be in position and prepared for your husband, you must allow God to heal you completely.

When you are not healed, this means that you are not whole and **an incomplete person does not have the capacity to become ONE with anyone**.

It was not until I made a conscious decision to be real with myself about the emotional-baggage I was carrying, that I was able to go before God and ask Him for help! Once I was in graduate school, I realized that all of the relationships I was in, failed. It did not matter how much I contributed and how much I gave of my time, effort, and love; the relationships did not result in marriage and did not end happily. The men that claimed they loved me, never asked to marry me. The guys I thought were wonderful had severe character flaws. The relationships I thought would turn me into a bride, only left me with a broken heart. Something *had* to change, and because I could not change the circumstances, could not change the man, I had to surrender and allow God to change ME. I needed God to fix me, mend me, and transform me. I needed God to HEAL me and FREE me of the emotional-baggage that was hindering me from experiencing pure joy and even recognizing true love. Quite honestly, the "love" that I was wrapped up in while in relationships was not true love at all. At the time, I did not know that I was not experiencing true love because the counterfeit love was serving its purpose of bringing what I thought was "healing" to my heart. In actuality, the counterfeit love was hurting my heart and soul even more.

Note this: You cannot expect the very one who broke your heart to heal your heart. No man [no human] can completely heal your life or heart; only the one who created your heart and gave you life CAN. This "only one" is GOD Himself.

You must decide today, not to hop into another relationship until you have surrendered yourself to God's healing process. Process is the key word. Process indicates *progression*, and progression signifies *time.* God can heal instantaneously and God can heal gradually. You must be committed to the process no matter the length of time.

Too often, women attempt to be in what they believe are fulfilling, long lasting, relationships with a man without being WHOLE (healed) and then they wonder why the relationship never leads to marriage. Is this you? Has this happened to you?

If you are wondering why your relationships never last and end with a happily-ever-after, may I suggest to you that there is a strong possibility that you are not HEALED and WHOLE?

It is not until you are made WHOLE that you can love authentically, trust undoubtedly, make decisions logically, and recognize pure love with certainty.

It is time out for blaming someone else as the reason for your relationships not working. I want you to consider YOU.

I was very open and honest with you in the beginning of this chapter about my experiences because I want you to see the power in BREAKING THE SILENCE and Being REAL with yourself and God.

If you want to be a WIFE, you need to be a woman who is WHOLE.

IT'S TIME TO GET REAL

Remember, **silence breeds secrets.**

Again, let me tell you this - **you cannot move past what you do not identify.**

As I coach women, I always encourage them to be honest with themselves and be vulnerable before themselves and before God. Many times, we have covered up our emotional baggage and hurt for so long that we forget we need to address the root of why we think, act, and/or conduct ourselves in relationships as we do. Remember I shared with you how after I was raped, because I had not intentionally dealt with the pain, the effects of the pain took control of me? Since I did not allow myself to surrender my heart before God so he could make me whole, every relationship I entered with a man was affected by my baggage. The way I conducted myself as I related to men was a direct result of my hurt, which I chose not to address.

My sister, I encourage you to BE REAL! Stop pretending that you are just fine when you are not. RIGHT NOW is the best time to allow God to heal you. **One of the greatest things you can do prior to marriage is allow God to make you WHOLE.**

Only God can heal the brokenness you were left with when that man was unfaithful to you, abandoned you, used you, abused you, misused, played with your emotions, and more.

Only God can heal your mind of depression, loneliness, guilt, regret, confusion, low self-worth, and more.

Only God can heal, restore, refresh, renew, and complete you!

ONLY GOD CAN HEAL YOU AND MAKE YOU WHOLE IN EVERY AREA OF YOUR LIFE

Your husband will **greatly** appreciate you for having taken the time BEFORE entering into marriage with him to allow God to HEAL and RENEW you.

Carrying emotional-baggage from the past as a result of you not being healed and made whole, will indeed affect your future marriage. You do not even have to ask me how I know! I am sharing this information with you *because* I know. Now, I THANK GOD for His HEALING POWER! He has done a MIGHTY work in me and in my MARRIAGE and I have written this book to help you better prepare and position yourself for what is to come.

As you continue reading this book, I want you to keep in mind that EVERYTHING you do (or do not do) before marriage has the ability to positively or adversely affect your future marriage. This is why (as you desire to be married) your preparation for marriage STARTS NOW. Actually, it has already begun. Everything you DO and experience PRIOR to marriage is preparing you for your spouse; therefore, in this season of your life, you want to make sure that your life is in alignment with God's plan and purpose for you.

The season you are in right now has purpose! During this time, BE REAL. BREAK THE SILENCE. BE HEALED. BE FREE! BE WHOLE!

#Ready4TheRing Plan of Action:
Be Healed & Be Whole

- ❖ Spend time with God in prayer and ask Him to help you identify the root cause of your actions, ideals, & decision making while in relationships and when dealing with men.
- ❖ Break the silence and verbally identify to God the emotional-baggage you have been carrying.
- ❖ Humbly and sincerely ask God to heal you from the inside-out. Ask Him to mend your brokenness and make you whole. You know what you need. Ask Him and believe by faith that it is done!
- ❖ Open up and talk with trusted family members. Often times we misperceive how they will respond, and we underestimate their ability to understand us and help us.

- ❖ Do not be afraid to seek out a licensed professional Christian counselor who will help you deal with trauma, grief, and other pain in a biblical manner.

- ❖ Take time to reflect and ask God to reveal to you where your unhealthy behaviors come from regarding your relationships with men. Give yourself permission to seek out a spiritual counselor, who can assist you as you process the root of the "learned behaviors" you have adopted.

- ❖ Be willing and committed to going through the healing process without interfering or 'helping' God. Know that everything will not be comfortable and the process may not always 'feel' good, but trust God, and know that the healing process will make you complete and WHOLE.

NOTES:

Chapter 2: Know Your Identity: You Are a Woman of Worth

❖ *Jewel of Wisdom:*

When you view yourself as God sees you, you will desire for yourself what God wants for you. Understanding the true essence of WHO you are, changes the pattern of WHAT you allow and what you accept. *#Ready4TheRing*

Have you ever had a moment when you think about someone who you were involved with in the past and you said to yourself or a friend, "I don't know *what* I was thinking?" I have actually said those very words while talking to one of my sister-friends several times! One afternoon she and I went on a brunch date and she began to tell me that she crossed paths with a guy I used to date while at a local university. She expressed how his demeanor was one of pride and how he was quite manipulative in relation to both his post-master's course work and his business. As we had girl talk over waffles that sunny day, while listening to her share information about him I could not help but think, w*hy in the world did I waste my time talking to him?* I had experienced the same arrogance and insincerity while dating him. *Why didn't I end that escapade before it even began?*

Often times when we look back at who we chose to date and allowed into our lives, we find that the person who we were connected to was not truly worth our time or attention. We may also begin to recognize that there were many warning signs and red flags we overlooked, which we should have paid attention to. If we had paid attention, we would have saved ourselves the hassle, time, regret, and emotional disillusionment.

In this chapter, I will not identify red flags; however, I am going to challenge you to identify the *real* reason why you ignored them. I want you to contemplate the basis for why you remained and/or are remaining in relationships that are not healthy for your spirit, mind, emotions, and soul.

WHY did you ignore the warning signs that were noticeable as a banner waiving in the air?

WHY did you talk to him even though he did not meet your basic standards?

WHY did you relate to someone who you now regret has experienced you in a way that only your husband should?

WHY did you give your all in a relationship when there were signals that lead you to question him and his motives?

WHY did you entertain him even though he has multiple children with many baby mamas?

WHY?

Yes, I am asking you to answer these heavily loaded questions. Yes, I want you to ask yourself many "why" questions in order to understand why you accepted less than what you truly deserved. I encourage you to explore just why you allowed certain things to happen in relationships you stayed in. Let me tell you, when I answered these questions about my own life, I had to face some not-so-pleasant truths about myself; but facing the truth allowed me to change my"truth".

So, why did I ignore warning signs that were as clear as a diamond? I overlooked the signs because I wanted to be connected with someone. His presence and his words gave me 'butterflies'. He said he loved me. He made me feel special. I wanted to feel prized, valued, desired, accepted, and I wanted to experience happiness. After all, is that too much to ask?

These are true thoughts I discovered I had once I intentionally 'dug deep' into my mind. Doing this type of reflection is a metacognitive process. In my study of psychology, "metacognition" refers to understanding and analyzing one's own cognitive processes. This is what I did, and now I strongly encourage you to do the same.

If you want to be married and position yourself to be found by God's perfect one for you, this means that you need to ask yourself those WHY questions above. What you do not need is more experiences in which you find yourself accepting less than what you truly deserve. You want to only engage in meaningful, honorable relationships that reflect your true worth.

For me, I found that the more I sought God in prayer, reflected on my patterns, and thought processes, my WHY questions began to be revealed.

So what was going on? This is what I found out about myself and you may be able to relate as you are honest with yourself as well.

WHY ACCEPTING "LESS" THAN THE BEST WAS SO EASY

I ignored warning signs because I desperately longed for the affection and attention that would make me feel complete and bring me joy.

I was seeking happiness in the experiences of admiration that others lavished upon me.

I was longing for a connection with others, men specifically, to validate my sense of value.

I was willing to compromise my standards and accept less than the best because I thought what men offered me was 'good enough' *for me.*

I remained connected with a man even after emotional abuse and physical misuse because I believed I needed him in order to experience fulfillment and love.

As you see, I was looking to a man to bring me happiness and contentment. I did not find contentment in being single. Being single was the last thing I wanted to be. My life's value and self-value was wrapped up in a man and what his presence <u>in</u> my life would add <u>to</u> my life.

Is this you? I know sometimes you "hate" being single, but what does that say about *you*? Whether you admit it or not, each time you complain about being single, it's like insulting your own value and the presence of God in your life. You do not *need* a man to enjoy your life and experience fulfillment. Now, don't misinterpret me, it's acceptable to desire a husband, but any time you compromise your own self just to have the presence of a man in your life, then your desire has become desperation. We are to be desperate for God and His will for our lives, not a man. So really quickly - let that "sink in" and do a "*heart check*".

THE REVELATION: KNOW YOUR WORTH

In short, my self-worth and self-value were lacking. In other words, I was not fully aware of MY OWN WORTH and MY OWN VALUE.

If I was FULLY aware of MY WORTH, I would not have accepted anything or anyone who did not match or compliment my greatness.

If I was FULLY aware of MY VALUE, I would not have ignored warning signs and red flags in order to feel loved and experience happiness.

If I was FULLY aware of my IDENTITY I would have been fully content with my life without having a man in my life.

I am being so very open and transparent with you because, I truly want you to know that you MUST be transparent too as you prepare yourself for marriage! You do not have to be transparent with me if you do not want to, but answer these questions for yourself!

This book is all about what you can do NOW, while single (unmarried) that will help you position your heart, mind, emotions, and spirit before marriage so that you can be the wife you desire to be!

I know you want to be married because you are reading this book, and I want you to understand you must know WHO you are: your VALUE and your WORTH before you are a wife!

I shared with you the following jewel of wisdom at the start of the chapter:

Understanding the true essence of WHO you are, changes the pattern of WHAT you allow and what you accept.

If you want to be married to God's best for you, you can no longer afford to be caught up in relationships and with people who treat you with less respect than you deserve, and with men who are not walking in step with God. The ONLY way you will no longer fall for the "okie-doke", smooth-talking man, or remain in relationships that lead to a dead-end is to KNOW YOUR IDENTITY in Christ! You must know your TRUE worth and value!

Of course many women would rather be in relationships that make them feel good than to admit they need some help in the area of their self-perception and image. How do I know? Again, I was one of them.

Here is a moment of truth: Are YOU one of them?

I know it does not make you *feel* good, nor does it give you much comfort to acknowledge that at one point you *have* or are currently struggling with "seeing yourself the way God sees you", but doing so will help you break the cycle of dead-end relationships, compromise, and more!

When you know, believe, and own the fact that God created you with greatness, brilliance, uniqueness, and that you are a VALUABLE TREASURE, then what you <u>accept</u> and what you *allow* in your life **will** change!

I really need you to know that you ARE Amazing!

You are Precious!

You are Wonderful!

You are Special!

You are a Royal Priesthood!

You are Extraordinary!

It is for this very reason that not every man needs access to you! It is for this very reason that you should not accept "any ole thing" when it comes to men. You are God's prized possession! He formed and created you with great purpose in mind! He designed you in *His* image, and you *know* just how GREAT God is! Just think about it, the sovereign, omnipotent, awesome, amazing, only true and living God of the universe created YOU!

You see, you *ARE* valuable and priceless!

Knowing your worth will cause you to raise the standard in your relationships and raise the standard for men to get to know you intimately.

When you know your worth, you will no longer accept being a side chick.

When you know your worth, you will no longer allow a man to cheat, beat, or mistreat you and you stay and accept it.

When you know your worth, you will not allow a man's compliments lead you to his bed.

When you know your worth, you will not be in relationships with men who keep you around without an official title or a ring.

When you know your worth, you will not make excuses for a man, but you will expect that a man meet your non-negotiable standards.

When you have something of value in your house, you don't just let people walk on it, touch it, or be around it without first making sure they are trustworthy and that they will be careful to respect your property. You make sure people treat it with care, you guard it, you protect it, and once you have evaluated their character and ability to honor your possession(s), then you let them near the valuables. If this is so, why then, do we allow men to have such easy access to *us* - a woman of great worth?

You are a Woman of Worth! You must know it! You must believe it! You must be it! You must own it!

Decide today to fully accept and believe that you are a Woman of Value! Know that you do not need a man to validate you. Know that you can experience a happy and fulfilling life as a single woman right now.

YOU are MORE than ENOUGH!

You *can* enjoy your life now!

You *are* worth the wait!

You *do not* have to settle!

God is more than able to send you a man who will honor you, and you will not have to compromise!

KNOW YOUR WORTH!

KNOW YOUR IDENTITY!

Walk in it, Live it, OWN it and be unapologetic aboutit!

#Ready4TheRing Plan of Action:
Know Your Identity

- On a piece of paper, list 10 or more of your positive attributes/characteristics.
- On another piece of paper, write 5-8 skills, talents, or gifts you possess.
- Search the scriptures and write down who God says you are. Who are you to Him? How did He create you to be? Here are a few to get you started! Ephesians 2:10| Psalm 139:14| 1 Peter 2:9| 1 Corinthians 5:17| Romans 8:37| Romans 8:17| Jeremiah 29:11.
- Now that you "see" just a glimpse of yourself on paper, read everything out loud. Finally write down what type of person would even deserve to have access to all of your greatness.

NOTES:

Chapter 3:
Renew Your Mind, Change Your Life

❖ *Jewel of Wisdom:*

Change happens when you renew your mind so you can think differently, and alter your habits so you can 'do' differently. It is not until you renew your mind and change your way of thinking, that you change your way of living and dating. In order to do this, you must rid yourself of the world's ideals of love & relationships, and put on the mind of Christ. #Ready4TheRing

Why do you need to renew your mind? Renewing your mind prior to marriage is necessary because your behaviors and actions are rooted in your mind's thought-processes and beliefs. You cannot enter into marriage with the same mindset you have as a single woman and expect to have a successful marriage. You will not be able to date in a way that leads to marriage with a mindset that is contrary to the Word of God. If you want to be in position to date in a God-honoring way and to be able to recognize true love *and* your husband - You must renew your mind!

Do you know that it is your thoughts and beliefs that dictate your actions, and influences your decisions in dating? Therefore, if your thoughts are not in alignment with GOD's Word, your actions will not be either. Likewise, if you have the mind of Christ, you will also have the power to please Him through your lifestyle *and* while in relationships.

While coaching women, I have noticed a consistent pattern which is one of the causes why many women do not experience true fulfillment in their relationships. I have found that many women have distorted views of love, relationships, and of themselves. Their beliefs about love and marriage are fictitious, unrealistic, and impractical. It has become common among women that our view of love and relationships is not grounded in the WORD nor the way GOD intended relationships and marriage to be. Instead, our perspective is based on the world's system, because we have allowed ourselves to be inundated by the world's perspective and values.

THE POWER OF MEDIA ON YOUR MIND

Are you a television fanatic? Maybe you're not a fanatic but you have a specific show that you "must see" each week. Clearing your schedule to faithfully watch your favorite "reality" shows, setting your DVR to record the latest sitcom, and being glued to the screen of movies either in your home or in a public theater may seem like pure entertainment, but these activities are having an effect on you. Each time you watch your favorite show, ideals from the media are being transmitted and stored in your mind. Constant exposure to these values, ethics, or lack thereof will influence your perspective and your life's desires. You must remember that Satan is "the prince of the power of the air" and he controls the media airways. With the media being such a powerful tool, why wouldn't he use this platform to infiltrate your mind in a very subtle way in the name of 'entertainment' or a 'brilliant storyline'? *This* is exactly what he is doing. As you watch and enjoy, unbeknownst to you, your perception about love becomes tainted and your view of relationships is being contaminated with ungodly ideals that appear to bring satisfaction.

This is why your mind must be renewed!

The media will have you believing such things as:

- Living with your mate prior to marriage is enjoyable and there is no consequence to doing so before marriage.

- It is flattering and attractive to gain the heart and affection of a man who is currently married but happens to be interested in you too.

- Cuddling, kissing, romance, and love is needed in your life in order for you to experience happiness and fulfillment.

- Having sex with the men you are in relationship with is suitable because the two of you are planning to get married.

- Make-up-sex is a satisfying experience, and while continuing to be in a relationship that is emotionally-unstable but sexually fulfilling, make-up sex demonstrates your true love and commitment to one another.

- Same-sex relationships are demonstrations of love similar to heterosexual relationships, and God approves this because God is love and we are *all* God's children.

These are just a *few* ideals that are being transmitted into your mind via the media. The more you allow these subliminal messages into your eye and ear gates, the more you become desensitized to the counterfeit messages being delivered. These messages are being conveyed everywhere from commercials, to cartoons, social media, music, radio, movies, video games, internet, and television.

CHANGE YOUR MINDSET

It is because of these messages that you have previously, or presently desire love and relationships which resemble the ideals above and more! It is because of the gratification and fulfillment these ideals portray, that you may have at some point believed they were acceptable. Please know that what you feed into your spirit and mind has the power to control your desires and cravings in this life.

This is why your mind must be RENEWED!

Without having a renewed mind, your mentality, desires, and focus are polluted and impure.

You will not desire the things of God when you are overtaken by the thoughts of indulgence and pleasures of this world.

Additionally, you will not be able to live a pure lifestyle and a “changed” life if your mind has not been renewed.

Moreover, you cannot effectively change your life, its outcomes, or be in position to be found by a Godly man, while

a.) maintaining a "worldly" perspective,

b.) holding onto worldly desires, or

c.) attempting to attain worldly aspirations in your personal life or relationships.

The bible lets us know that we are IN the WORLD, but NOT *of* the world. This means that although we live in the world, we must not allow the world and its ideology to be in us. We must not live by the same guiding principles. We are to live by God's Word. The only way we can make sure we are not *of* the world, is to live by the WORD [the Word of God; the Holy Bible] and to renew our mind.

Have you tried over and over again to "stop having sex" but you continue to find yourself in a man's bed or him in yours?

Have you said that you will leave your ex alone but he seems to make you weak and his words cause you to go against your better judgment every time?

Have you been curious about lesbian relationships and have secretly considered trying it out?

Have you been dating a married man without shame because you believe that he just may leave his wife for you?

Have you found yourself debating whether or not it's "okay" for a couple to live together before marriage when this was a topic in which you would never even consider without guilt before?

May I suggest to you that you are having these thoughts because you do not fully have on the mind of Christ? You have completely allowed the enemy to reign in your mind. My sister, you must guard your mind and not even let a hint of immoral thoughts enter in. You need to cast down those thoughts and the ones you have that I have not even mentioned. Only you and God know the impure thoughts that are in your mind. Satan knows that if he attacks your mind and perception, he can influence your decisions and cause you to abandon righteousness and God's truths. Know that any desires you have that are contrary to the Word of God are not from God, but strictly from the enemy of your soul. The tingles you get in your flesh and the desires you have to want to engage in activities that do not glorify God are sinful. Don't be fooled. You cannot dip and dab in the world's ideals of relationships and love and then expect for God to send his best, your husband. It does not work that way.

Stop giving in to your F-L-E-S-H. It's time for your mind to be RENEWED!

If you are indulging in love and demonstrating it in the same manner as the world - this is the direct result of allowing yourself to be consistently exposed to the world's ideals and a lack of indulgence of the Word of God.

Today, I am encouraging you to RENEW YOUR MIND! When you renew your mind, you change your life!

Your thoughts will change.

Your desires will change.

Your aspirations will change.

Your focus will change.

Your standards will change.

Your decisions will change.

Your actions will change.

Your habits will change.

Your character will change.

Your relationships will change.

YOU will *be* changed!

HOW TO RENEW YOUR MIND

I know you may be very familiar with the passage of scripture below, but I am inviting you to explore these verses with me. I pray that God speaks to you as you read and meditate on this.

Romans 12:1-2 (NIV) says, *"Therefore, I urge you, brothers and sisters, in view of God's mercy, tooffer your bodies as a living sacrifice, holy and pleasing to God—this is your true and proper worship. 2 Do not conform to the pattern of this world, but be transformed by the renewing of your mind. Then you will be able to test and approve what God's will is—his good, pleasing and perfect will."*

In this passage of scripture we see that "renewing your mind" comes as a result of a person no longer conforming to the pattern of this world.

Previously in this chapter, I listed just a few of *many* patterns and beliefs that people in this earthly 'world' live by. The apostle Paul who wrote this book of the Bible is saying to no longer abide by the same principles of the world. That is one step to renewing your mind.

Before he says not to conform anymore, he urges all believers to "offer your bodies as a living sacrifice". This lets us know that God is not *making* anyone present their body, but He wants the people of God to *willingly* give their body to Him as a sacrifice. This means that we should give up the desires of our mind and our flesh, present ourselves to God, and forsake living according to the world's views. When we do this we "transform" or change our lives because our mind is being/has been renewed. Renewed means converted; to make new-again.

So, again I encourage you to renew your mind! NOW is the time for you to completely give yourself to God (sacrifice) and turn away from the desires, mindset, and ideals that are of the world. Turn away from that which is contrary to God's word so that you can experience a change in your life and have a renewed mind!

Here's the good news! The scripture points out that once you are *transformed by the renewing of your mind* "Then you will be able to test and approve what God's will is". You see, renewing your mind has a strong benefit! It is when you have done all of the above in order to transform and renew your mind that you are actually *able* to know, test, and align yourself with God's perfect will! This is awesome! If you have ever struggled with knowing and discerning God's will, perhaps it was because you were not fully submitting yourself unto Him and you were conforming to the world. You must know, as you transform your lifestyle by renewing your mind - you will be tested. It is through the test that you will be able to prove God's good, acceptable, and perfect will when you consistently pursue God and His presence.

Wow!

Now why *wouldn't* you want to renew your mind?

As you desire to be married, renewing your mindset and knowing God's will for your life is essential. Marriage is no play thing. Marriage is a holy institution designed by God which unites one man and one woman together for as long as they both shall live. Marriage is a sacred God-honoring commitment and should not be entered into lightly. You will need to know His will when it comes time for you to discern whether or not a man who you *think* is "The One" is *actually* The One.

I always say that in life, we prepare for many things: vacation, a job interview, a night out, the holidays, etc. Why would you prepare any less for your future marriage? You need to do what it takes to position yourself to receive all that God has for you! Know that *better women make better wives.* Start positioning and preparing yourself for marriage 'Right Now' by RENEWING YOUR MIND. Renewing your mind today will change your life!

#Ready4TheRing Plan of Action:
Change The Way You Think

- Take some time to reflect upon the ideals about love and relationships which have become part of your mindset/beliefs/guiding principles that were influenced by mainstream culture and/or media. Write it down.

❖ Using the word of God, write down a counter principle and/or scripture that represents righteousness and holiness.

❖ Ask God to forgive you for abiding by and/or believing the principles of the world.

❖ Spend time in prayer with God and with a sincere heart, present your body to Him as a living sacrifice. In other words, make the decision to subdue (tame) your fleshly desires to maintain a mind of purity, which according to his Word, pleases God. Renounce and forsake the ways of the world and commit to conforming to HIM.

❖ Ask God to transform your life and renew your mind.

❖ Spend time meditating on His word and praying daily so you may be able to *prove what is the good, and acceptable, perfect will of God.* Making a point to set time aside to spend with God is YOU taking the initiative to invite Him into your personal space. Spending time with God can look like a variety of activities other than reading your Bible. For example, following a devotional book with scriptures, a Bible App on your phone, taking quiet time to give God thanks for your day, sharing with God the desires of your heart, praying for others and their needs, all the while - asking God to provide you with revelation from your reading and quiet time spent with Him.

NOTES:

Chapter 4: **Think Like a Man, Live Like a Wife**

❖ *Jewel of Wisdom:*

Being his woman, does not necessarily mean you will be his wife. If you give your body, time, resources, and intimacy without a marital commitment, what's left to give once a commitment is made? What can he have which he has not already had access to? What can you give as a wife that you have not already given as his woman? What would be the benefit in him marrying you? There is none. With this in mind, you must hold back. Do not give so much of yourself. When you give less, in the end, you will get more. It is <u>your</u> actions that help determine his corresponding actions. It is time to be wise. Think like a man and carry yourself like a woman who truly wants to be a wife. <u>#Ready4TheRing</u>

I must be quite honest with you. Prior to getting married, I would not have thought that "giving less will get you more". However, this is now a jewel of wisdom that I share with my clients who desire to be married. Like you, I actually thought the opposite at one point in my life. I believed that if I demonstrated *just how much* I loved him, *just how much* I cared, and if I showed him *just how much* I wanted to be with him, then for sure he would not have a reason not to marry me. In one previous relationship, I was doing everything I knew to do, everything I could do, and getting a ring would have made me that happiest woman on earth! Just like many women, I was sold on the "fact" that if I supported him, met his needs, gave my all, was faithful, and completely committed to him that he would marry me, right? WRONG. Yes, I was wrong, and if you actually look at your own track record with men (and are *honest* with yourself) you will see that you too have been deceived. As a coach, I have had many women say to me "I just don't know what else I can do" or "I just don't know what else I could have done" and "I don't know what I could have done differently, I did everything I could". These are women just like you and I who are Christian, educated, and goal-oriented women who have expressed their sentiments while explaining to me how they could not understand why the man they were with, did not marry them.

Have you experienced this same situation in your life? You may even be experiencing this right now as you are reading this book. It happens quite frequently that a woman is emotionally hurt because the man who they were with left them broken-hearted instead of making them a bride, even after they did everything they "knew" to do. If you have been in a relationship and hoped it would lead to marriage, and it did not, you certainly are not alone. Now before I allow you to go into a pity party or begin to think that all of us just happened to be involved with men who were "no good"- let me stop you. I will not allow you to place all the blame on the men without challenging you to take responsibility for your own actions. I don't mean to be harsh, but I had to do this same thing for myself. You must recognize that you share in the responsibility of why your ex did not make you his wife. I know, *it's tight, but it's right.*

UNDERSTAND A MAN BUT DON'T BE *LIKE* ONE

You must understand that men and women are two distinctly different beings. Men and women do not even think on the same sides of their brain. We do not share identical perspectives and therefore we cannot continue to be in relationships with men without ever taking a moment to suppose the manner in which a man thinks. Understanding how a man thinks, and what he wants in a wife, will help you in the way you handle yourself while in relationship with one. The title of this chapter is *Think Like a Man, Live Like a Wife.* Before you get upset that I am telling you to think like someone you are not, let me explain what I mean and bring clarity to the topic of this portion of the book.

As a Christian, we are to live in accordance with God's Holy Bible. In God's Word, he tells his sons and daughters *'Do not be yoked together with unbelievers. For what do righteousness and wickedness have in common?'* (2 Corinthians 6:14). His Word also says in Proverbs 12:4 that *a wife of noble character is her husband's crown.* Because *you* are a follower of Christ, you ought to desire to be married to a man who is a disciple of Christ as well, right? You should want a man of whom you will be equally yoked, right? So now you *must* understand that this type of man is actually looking for a wife who is living her life in a pure and honorable way. *This* man of God, because he is after God's heart will not want to be yoked with a woman who is not living righteously. He also will want a wife who will be his crown, because she is of noble character. Just to clarify, a noble woman is someone who has high morals and ideals; this woman has personal qualities that people admire; this woman is one who is d e e m e d worthy of high respect. When I use the term *Think Like a Man,* I am specifically challenging you to consider the perspective and viewpoint of a MAN of GOD who is striving to please Him in all areas of his life, and particularly desires a woman who will be his *good thing.* So now that you understand this, I want you to give considerable thought to whether or not a man of God, a disciple of Christ, would delight in being connected with *you* as his wife.

It is time to *think* like a God-honoring man right now.

Would a man of God who is looking for his *crown*, a woman of honor, be pleased with the woman you are now, the woman you were, and who you are becoming?

Are you truly a woman of good character?

Would a man after God's own heart be disappointed with the decisions that *you've* made while in relationships prior to meeting him, or would he have the privilege of feeling *honored* by becoming ONE with you in marriage?

You see, as a disciple of Christ, a man of God will desire to become ONE with a woman who is in alignment with the characteristics the bible shares that a wife should have, and how they should be. This man will want to marry a woman who will be his crown. Let me share with you more about what this means, so you can recognize the significance behind doing an honest self-evaluation upon finishing this chapter. There are a few expressions of "crown" in the bible, some by which symbolize the concept of consecration and exaltation. A second term for crown indicated the presence of honor in the Old Testament. In some cases, the bible pictured the **reception of honor** as one who **entered into a special position**. Wives were crowned with honor to show their new status. In other cases, the crown indicated the presence of honor as a **cause for glory and joy**. These are more metaphorical uses. So a **good wife** is a **crown** to her husband (Proverbs 12:4). Essentially this denotes that a wife should be the cause for glory and joy unto her husband. Because they have entered into marriage, the husband is a recipient of honor because he has entered into a special position of husband, with her as his wife.

So my question to you is this:

If your husband were to find you today, would he be honored and experience joy because of his union with you?

THE STORY OF RUTH: A LESSON LEARNED

As it has already been stated, a man of God would be honored by joining himself with a woman of noble character. Let's go back to the story of Ruth and Boaz. I assume you are familiar with this story, and that you may have even asked God to send you your "Boaz". As you know, Ruth was taking care of her mother-in-law Naomi after both of their husbands had died. Ruth actually went back to Naomi's hometown to live with her and be her caretaker. One day, while Ruth was in the fields, gathering left-over grain, she happened to be in a field belonging to Boaz. I encourage you to read the book of Ruth in the Old Testament of the bible for the whole story, however the part I want to emphasize right now is found in Ruth, chapter 2, verse 5 which states,

"Boaz asked the overseer of his harvesters, "Who does that young woman belong to?"

In this verse, it is evident that Ruth caught the attention of Boaz, and he wanted to know more about her.

In the following verse the man responded by saying, *"She is the Moabite who came back from Moab with Naomi."*

Further in the chapter, after Boaz tells Ruth that she will be taken care of, he makes sure she has all the food she needs, and that she is protected from harm. Ruth asks Boaz in verse 10 *"Why have I found such favor in your eyes that you notice me—a foreigner?"*

Boaz replied by telling her that he heard ***good*** things about her! In essence when he asked his servants (the men around) who she was, they had nothing but positive and favorable things to say about her. They gave her compliments and spoke about her good character because she was taking care of Naomi. Do you see the BIG AHA-moment here? Boaz wanted to be with Ruth because she was a woman of distinction and honor!

Now, ask yourself:

* Am *I* a woman of great HONOR?

* If a man who was interested in me asked other men about *me*, would he hear favorable information?

Would those men say that you are *easy* or *loosey-goosey?* Would they say you are the church girl who has everyone fooled into believing you are astute, but they've heard what you do behind closed doors after you leave the altar? Would they say you are a preacher in public, but a freak in private? Side note: Yes, my sister - men DO talk, and though you may keep secrets, there are some men who do not! They may share with their boys publically what you thought would remain secret.

It is very significant that Boaz's men had nothing but positive things to say about Ruth. *This* is what you should want for yourself! So, ask yourself - *Would my potential future husband believe that I am a woman of great character, or would I have a bad reputation amongst others? What would other men say about me?*

I know these are *profound* questions; they are REAL questions you need to ask yourself, and the answers may reveal to you that you need to truly align every part of your life to God's word, starting today!

My sister, here is what I need you to remember: The decisions you make today, affect your life tomorrow. How you handle yourself while in relationships with men prior to marriage, has the potential to affect the relationship with your future husband. Some decisions you make, may cause a man not to consider marrying you. YES - just like we have standards, many men DO too! Although you are single (unmarried) right now, you cannot afford to live carelessly, loosely, and un-intentionally. You MUST live like a woman who desires to be married, understanding that the type of man you actually want to be married to, is one who will want a wife who is honorable!

NOW is the time for you to start aligning your decisions while single with your true desire to be married. This means that you will have to sacrifice the desires of your flesh to have sex, to not be a smart-mouth, and to not date haphazardly. Break your selfish habits. Learn how to communicate. Do not compromise your value for the love of a man. You must crucify your flesh if you truly want to be found as a *good thing* to your husband and be considered as your husband's crown.

BECOMING WIFE- MATERIAL

Remember, a Christian man, will desire to marry a woman who is in alignment with what a wife should be. Let's explore what the bible says about a WIFE.

✓ **Proverbs 18:4** *A wife of noble character is her husband's crown, but a disgraceful wife is like decay in his bones.*

I would like to believe that I have expounded on this enough that you understand the significance in being a noble woman, so let's examine the second part of the verse which says: a *disgraceful wife is like decay in his bones.*

Someone who is disgraceful is "shameful; scandalous". To disgrace is to cause (someone or something) to lose respect or become unworthy of respect or approval. The verse says that this type of woman is decay in a man's bones. You know that when something decays it is slowly broken down. So when a wife's lifestyle is shameful and when a woman lives scandalously, she is a disgrace to her husband and causes him to break down slowly inside. Certainly, I hope that you do not want to have this effect on your future husband. Instead you want to be his crown! This means right now you need to live like a wife! Be a woman of noble character. Be a woman of honesty, integrity, faithfulness, respect, trust, and distinction.

✓ **Proverbs 31:10** *A wife of noble character who can find? She is worth far more than rubies.*

Once again, the bible describes a wife as someone of noble character. I always remember being told that when God mentions the same thing twice or more, He is trying to get your attention. Hopefully, He has yours now! In addition to being noble, the verse says her worth is more than rubies! You know rubies are expensive! So, a man who marries this type of woman recognizes her worth! He recognizes who she is; who God created her to be! Let me tell you this, a man is aware of a woman's worth based on how she exudes her own worth! This means that a woman herself must know WHO she is and how great she is! We have already addressed "identity" in a previous chapter. Before you are finished reading this book, my prayer is that you truly know and believe that you are valuable! You are special! You are wonderful! You are a woman of purpose! You are made in God's image! You are priceless! When you know *who* you are, a man is able to know who you are, because your value will shine bright like a diamond! *This* is what will actually get a diamond ring on your finger too!

- ✓ **Proverbs 25:24** *Better to live* on a *corner* of the *roof* than share a house with a quarrelsome wife.

WHOA! Now *this* is serious! Here's another question to ponder: If you and your future husband were married right now, would he be on the rooftop? Would your mouth have caused him not to desire to be near you at all, to the point that he leaves the house? Many women do not like to admit that they have a "smart mouth" however whether they admit it or not, for some, it *is* true. Are you full of sarcasm? Do you always have to have the last word? Do the words you speak, impart life or do they tear down? Men need to feel respected at all times. Did you know that your words can indeed speak louder than your actions? You cannot talk to a man recklessly and expect that he honor you. You cannot talk to a grown man like a boy and think that he believes you respect him. It does not work like that. It doesn't matter even if you all are having a 'heated discussion' (i.e. argument). You cannot use that as an excuse to be in his face, have an over-powering tone, or curse him out. You are a Christian woman right? So you *must* know that *a gentle answer turns away wrath, but a harsh word stirs up anger* - Proverbs 15:1. It is time to start living out that word, instead of just *knowing* the verse!

I'll admit, during the first year of marriage with my husband, he was ready to live on the roof! It was bad. I did not bridle my tongue and sometimes my words were not edifying. When my husband brought this to my attention, I did not want to believe him, which resulted in me 'giving him a piece of my mind' some more. Though I was telling him I loved him, those words meant nothing because I was not respecting Him. I had to ask God to help me and to cleanse me of my deteriorating speech! The awesome thing about God is that he is faithful and He hears our prayers! Once I *submitted* to Him, asked Him to help me change my attitude, *prayed* daily, and *crucified* my flesh, then I began to change. I asked Him to empower me so that I could be a better wife to my husband and He did! Listen, it is not too early for *you* to also examine your attitude and disposition! Both the position of your heart and your mental disposition determines your speech patterns. If you know you need to work on 'your mouth' ask God to help you now rather than waiting until later. Then submit to his cleansing process. Your future husband will definitely appreciate it!

- ✓ **1 Corinthians 7:2** *But since sexual immorality is occurring, each man should have sexual relations with his own wife, and each woman with her own husband.*

A woman who is a *good thing* is one who does not engage in sexual activities with a man whom she is not married to. Instead she saves herself for her own husband. This scripture complements the verses above about being noble. I cannot stress to you enough that your actions right now while single can positively or adversely affect your future marriage. As a single woman, I desired to be married, but I never gave a thought about how my decisions to have sex pre-martially would affect the relationship between myself and my husband. Again, many married women would not admit or share that their sexual past has affected their marriage, but I will tell you the truth - mine has. Many leaders in the church do not address the psychological impact on a husband or wife when either one or both of the spouses have engaged in premarital sex. The church typically focuses on telling singles not to have sex because it is sin, and the consequences addressed are limited to STDs and pregnancy. While these reasons for saving sex until marriage are very important, we must also keep in mind that God ordained marriage as a safe haven for sex, and doing so outside of the confines of marriage, potentially presents issues and concerns within a marriage that could have been avoided.

This is why I will continue to remind you that you must think futuristically and no longer believe that the choices you make while single will only affect you. Start thinking about your future husband and honor him by living a pure lifestyle now.

Amongst many corresponding effects, when you have sex before marriage, you put yourself and your husband at risk for making comparisons and questioning the level of your sexual sincerity. Having sex outside of marriage can cause regret, shame, and even ill-feelings in relation to specific sexual activities. The affect of pre-marital sex on your part and/or on the part of your future husband can present *these* and more challenging issues in your marriage. It is very uncommon to discuss these silent, yet prevalent consequences of premarital sex, but I need you to know they DO exist. I personally know many engaged and married couples who are facing these challenges, and through the power of God my husband and I continue to overcome them every day!

In sharing all of this, I will also testify that GOD IS GREATER than any problems you and/or your future spouse may face as a result of sexual impurity before marriage. God is able to bring reconciliation, He is able to renew hearts, He is able to bring about forgiveness, rebuild trust, transform minds, and restore marital joy and fulfillment! God is simply amazing!

My sister, note this disclaimer: Although God can restore you and/or your future husband, do not let this be a reason to continue in sexual sin. The bible clearly states that we must not continue in sin so that grace may abound! You do not want to experience the negative consequences of your actions once you become married, when you could have prevented consequences by keeping your legs closed and living pure before God. God can endow you with keeping power! Guard your eye and ear gates so that you will not be tempted and drawn away by your own lustful desires! Know that sex before marriage is sin and sin has consequences. You may have avoided pregnancy, and you may not have contracted an STD as consequence to your sin, but sexual immorality can affect your life, your husband, and marriage in other ways. So stop while you are ahead. Do not add another number to your list. Honor God with your body now, so that you can honor your husband later. Commit to purity and forsake sexual immorality! You *and* your husband will appreciate it in the future!

✓ **Ephesians 5:22** *Wives, submit yourselves to your own husbands as you do to the Lord.*

That's right! A wife is a woman who possesses the Godly character trait of submission. I'll be the first to say that I strongly disliked the thought of submission. But now, I love submission! Submission means that I get to come up under the leadership of my husband as he leads us to accomplish the mission God has set forth for our marriage. Let me make this clear, submission does not mean I am being controlled or that I am weak, and it does not mean that I do not have a voice. Submission *does* mean that I trust my husband and as he follows Christ, I am committed to following him because he is the leader of our household. Any other order of submission that deviates from Christ as head, the husband following Him, and my husband leading me - is out of order. Please know that a woman should not be leading her husband. A woman must know how to allow her husband to lead. Submission would not be a problem if you marry someone who is a true follower of Christ. This is why you must be careful and intentional about **who** you date.

Listen - dating, courting, and engagement is what leads to marriage. If you do not see yourself being able to submit to him in the future, why are you allowing yourself to be with him now? While you are single, you must still think *futuristically*. Have no doubt that while you are dating, your potential future husband is watching you. He is observing your character and *sizing* you up to determine if he could be with you for life. That is why you must start carrying yourself as a woman with wife characteristics now. If he does not see you as someone who will trust him to lead as He follows God or does not see you as a noble woman, he will not make you his wife later.

THE MAN PARADOX: LESS IS MORE

Before closing this chapter, I want to go back to the jewel of wisdom I shared in the beginning.

Being his woman, does not necessarily mean you will be his wife. If you give your body, time, resources, and intimacy without a marital commitment, what is left to give once a commitment is made? What can he have which he has not already had access to? What can you give as a wife that you have not already given as his woman? What would be the benefit in him marrying you? There is none. With this in mind, you must hold back. Do not give so much of yourself. When you give less, in the end, you will get more. It is <u>your</u> actions that help determine his corresponding actions. It is time to be wise. Think like a man and carry yourself like a woman who truly wants to be a wife. #Ready4TheRing

If you were hoping your man would propose and he did not, I know it's easy to blame everything on him, but throughout this chapter I have been challenging you to consider you. In addition to the wife characteristics shared above, which will attract a man to you, you also want to leave a man with a reason to marry you. I am not saying to convince him; however I am saying to be careful not to give so much of yourself that you subtract his motivation to marry you. The ultimate way to lose his enthusiasm is to give him all the benefits of having a wife before he makes you his wife.

Take a moment to think like a man. If a man has access to free sex, home-cooked meals, laundry service, child care; If you are sharing bank accounts, car keys, house keys, and bodies; If you do the administrative work to support his vision/business, you spend your every free moment with him, and you are willing to spend your last dime on him, all without a marital commitment, why would he need to marry you? He is getting all the benefits of a wife from his woman! Giving your all to him, has taken away ALL of his incentives to marry you!

If you've had the same question as many other women *"What else could I have done for him to marry me?"* Sadly, the answer is - NOTHING. You've already allowed yourself to be too vulnerable. You gave too much of yourself. There was not anything else you could have done to get him to marry you. You had already given him everything. From this day forward, remember that: Less Is More!

After investing so much of yourself into a relationship without a return, I agree, is very hurtful; however, I must encourage you to accept responsibility for *your* actions. You have to identify your own mistakes in order for you to recognize that you need to change your habits. Now that you are aware of your downfall, make a vow not to give yourself away to a man completely until you have revelation from God that he is your husband AND this man has made you his wife through a marital commitment. Right now, I encourage you to give yourself away to GOD completely. Wrap yourself up in Him, be ONE with Him. At the appointed time you will have the opportunity to be a wife, until then remember you are the bride of Christ. Focus on giving your all to Him!

HEAR IT FROM THE SOURCE: A MAN'S PERSPECTIVE

So, I have shared a load of information with you, but I also want you to gain perspective from a few men! What better way to understand a man, than to hear directly from one! I do not ever want you to say you "didn't know" how a man thinks.

I was asked the question below by a lady on Facebook one day. After I gave her my response, I posted the question on my Facebook page to offer insight to her and other women like you! The question was:

What can a Christian woman do to attract a Christian man?

Here are some responses from a few men who answered!

- "Honesty is the best policy. No game playing, be the woman God created you to be, not who you think you should be or what you THINK he (the man) wants you to be. Now I'm not saying not to make a good impression, but don't make a FAKE impression either." – *Michael Banks, single man*

- "The best and only way for a woman to attract the right man is to implement and maintain abstinence, value her time, have loyalty and a great personality. All an honorable man wants is a good woman who's worth the best love & devotion." – *Jermaine Johnson, single man*

- "Be who you are...if the Spirit of Christ is in you BOTH, then the SPIRIT will take it from there. Again, I say, be who you REALLY are...not what anyone tells you or suggest you SHOULD be, but be who and what you are." – *Minister Charles Collier, happily married man*

- "Being open and honest about spirituality not your sexuality. Putting God first!" – *Joshua Hicks, single man*

- "A woman whose life is "in order" as far as her relationship with Jesus Christ, career, work ethic, commitment to Biblical principles, dating habits, submission to Godly authority in her life, etc. in many instances is attractive to a Kingdom minded man." - *Dr. Julian Hunt, happily married man*

- "Ok, I'm going to keep it real. Christian men are men. As with other men, our attention is grabbed by good looks and what we like physically, period. This does not change because I'm saved. That being said, modest sexiness is attractive. Once you have our attention, you must have substance, a friendly smile, smooth conversation, and has her own life with her own world-view. Last and not least, a life of service to God. I always tell Shalesha Moore (my wife) that nothing turns me on more than watching her serve God." – *Minister Evans Moore, happily married man*

FINAL THOUGHTS: LIVE LIKE A WIFE

The overarching theme that I want you to remember from this chapter is that your behavior right now while single, should be that of a wife. Keep this in mind. You do not attract what you desire. **You attract what you present & portray.** If you present that you are loose by being overly flirtatious, too willing to spend time at his house, and you give too much of yourself - then you will attract a man who is spiritually immature and looking for a fun time without a total commitment. If you display respect by having boundaries and standards, then you will attract a man who is looking for a respectable and noble woman. Be a woman of respect. Know your identity because when you know who you are, a man will know how to treat you. If you want to attract a husband, your lifestyle must be that of a wife. Christian men want a woman who is noble and wise, not a woman who has gone wild. Remember, giving less of yourself to other men, including the man you are with, positions you to experience more with your future husband. Make it your goal to be a woman who can become her husband's crown.

#Ready4TheRing Plan of Action:
Become A Woman of Noble Character

- ❖ Think and reflect on these questions. Identify and write down your reasoning and rationale to the following question: Would a man of God who is looking for his *crown* (a woman of honor), be pleased with the woman you are now, the woman you were, and who you are becoming?

- ❖ Think, reflect, and be honest with yourself and God. Write down the answers to these questions: Are you truly a woman of good character? Why or why not? Would a man after God's own heart be disappointed with the decisions that *you've* made while in relationships prior to meeting him? Would a man have the privilege of feeling *honored* by becoming ONE with you in marriage? Why or why not? If not, write an action plan for how you will transform your lifestyle.

- ❖ A moment of honesty: Think from the perspective of men who you have been in relationship with, and answer this question: If my husband were to find *me* today and then asked other men about *me*, what would he find out?

- ❖ Read Proverbs 18:4| Proverbs 31:10 | Proverbs 25:24 | 1 Corinthians 7:2 | Ephesians 5:22 | Identify the characteristics you are strong in.

Where are you lacking? Write down your prayer to God. Ask God to mature you in that area. Study more about that characteristic in the bible. Commit to your own personal and spiritual growth.

- ❖ Identify the changes you need to make in your personal life: how you will carry yourself differently, and what you will do differently in your next relationship in order to display your worth. Write down your goal and plan.

NOTES:

Part 2

Align Your Decisions With Your Desires

Chapter 5: Break Up With False Hope

❖ *Jewel of Wisdom:*

Being more in love with the "idea" of love rather than actually experiencing true love will cause you to be committed to false hope. It is time to break up with false hope and shake your clouded emotions, feelings, and fairytale endings so you can clearly see the facts. Knowing the truth will set you free from the emotional-bondage of false hope. #Ready4TheRing

Are you committed to *false hope*? I describe ***false hope*** as a strong aspiration for a *happily-ever-after* future with a man despite all the odds and evidence that suggest otherwise. *False hope* is anticipating something that has a strong chance of not happening, but you ignore the facts, and insist on believing your wish. *False hope* is what causes you to remain committed to your desires even though the man you are with may not be fully committed to *you*. *False hope* is the aspiration that keeps many women in relationships well past their expiration date and causes women to fall prey to a man who can very easily take advantage of them. False hope breeds desperation. Once you have made up in your mind that you will "do whatever it takes" to make your dream come true, despite the odds, and even his lack of commitment, then you have allowed your feelings to override the very present facts that exist.

Of course, no woman ever believes they are married to false hope, because during the season of false hope you are in "la-la land". You are in an infatuation stage. You are "living in a dream" and it is at this point that no one can tell you anything. You get upset when someone tells you to "slow down" in your relationship. You despise anyone who tries to shed some light on the character traits of the man you are with. You think everyone who tries to share their wisdom and input about your relationship is "jealous". You ignore the warning signs that are present. You overlook his downfalls, and you decide that you will stick with him because you want the end result of being his wife, being his woman, getting a ring, or even having his baby. You want *what* you want, no matter the cost and no matter the consequence because truthfully, you do not believe there are any. You become oblivious to the truth that you are forsaking the facts about him *and* your relationship in order to satisfy your feelings.

FALSE HOPE IN ACTION - TAKE 1

While I was single, I lived by *false hope* a number of times. I'm sharing my life with you because I want you to know that you are not alone in what you are dealing with as a single (unmarried) woman. My goal is to help you break some of the unhealthy behaviors which are hindering you from being in position to be found by your true husband. Living by false hope is indeed a habit you must break! Among many times, there are two specific times that I remember being completely overtaken by my false hope.

The first time was when I was a senior in high school and I wanted to have the story of marrying my "high school sweetheart" like I witnessed on television and in the movies. I wanted this desperately, even if it meant I would need to lower my standards to get what I wanted. My boyfriend at the time told me he wanted to marry me one day. He made a promise that he would propose to me in a specific year. This was like music to my ears and I believed him with all my heart, but the problem was the year of proposal was planned as the year we would graduate from college. As 18 year olds, we had not quite experienced life yet. We just graduated from high school and were preparing for college. I was the recipient of a tuition scholarship to a state university; however he was accepted to a university in the south thousands of miles away. Due to the circumstance of being miles away, he suggested we break up so that we would not prevent one another from fully enjoying the college experience. I reluctantly agreed, and with that, we planned to continue our relationship with an unofficial title, and made an agreement that whenever we came home for the holidays and semester breaks, we would be "back together again".

As I reflect upon this situation, I was so *in love* with the idea of *marrying my high school sweetheart* that I deceived myself into thinking that giving each other space and reuniting during the breaks was a pure love experience. I was married to false hope as I believed that this pattern would work for four years of college, possibly more, and then we would magically get married. I believed he loved me and that he would indeed propose to me one day. I chose to believe that "absence would make our hearts grow fonder", while I secretly hoped no one else would ever catch his eye like I had. Ending our relationship was painful. Inside I was afraid that we may not get back together. Really, what were the chances? He was thousands of miles away. We did not know what would happen in the future, but I had a tight grip on false hope. I refused to believe the unfavorable possibilities. I *knew* he was going to *sow his wild oats* while we were not officially together but because I wanted to be with him, I accepted the lifestyle with the attitude that *he had better not end up with a baby*. In my mind, *this* was where I would finally draw the line and not marry him. I knew I did not want to deal with baby-mama-drama. Moreover, I had always dreamt of my husband and I having our first child together.

I know, right now you may be thinking that I was *crazy* to believe that he and I would reunite after college and marry one another. I am actually laughing at myself as I am sharing this story with you because my beliefs about the entire situation were very foolish! Yes, I was *crazy in love,* and he had me thinking crazily too! Some may say I was "young and dumb", but this still encompasses living by false hope. That's the essence of false hope! It makes you foolish because you choose to live by your feelings and not by reality.

I am sure you can imagine how this story ended. In short, exactly what I feared would happen, did happen. During our sophomore year of undergraduate school, he called me to break the news about a girl's pregnancy and he was the father. I was completely devastated. I thought he loved me. I believed his word when he said he wanted to marry me. I had even laid aside my high standards and expectations of him so that my dreams could become reality.

It's very easy to notice right now that I was irrational and lacked common sense and good judgment. It was not until many years later that I became able to recognize the truth; marriage with him was unlikely, especially since we were not even in a committed relationship with one another. Why did I hang onto him? Why didn't I relinquish a desire that had a strong chance of not happening? You know why? It was because I decided to allow my feelings to guide my decisions and thoughts, even if it meant that I was being unwise by choosing not to recognize the facts. The fact was, we were young, and I should not have attempted to live according to "the girls in the movie". The fact was that we were experiencing "puppy love" and not a mature, sincere, pure love. The fact was that although I wanted to maintain a long distance relationship, he did not. The fact was that I devalued myself and did not live as a young woman who truly recognized what she deserved. The truth was I was committed to an idea of love that I wanted to become my reality but he was not even fully committed to me. You see, I was holding onto false hope.

FALSE HOPE IN ACTION – TAKE 2

I will share another example of a time when I was living by false hope. Again, I challenge you to examine your own life to determine whether you have lived by false hope too, or to identify whether you are right now. Either way, it is always necessary to know the mistakes you have made in your life both past and present, so that you do not repeat them in the future. Take time to identify similar thought patterns that you might have now, that were present in my false hope cases, because false hope syndrome tends to deceive one into thinking the concept of false hope is itself artificial. However, once you recognize it in others, you can liken their experience to your own.

Another occurrence of living by false hope took place as I was a single professional woman. *Yes my sister, living by false hope is not just a teenage habit; as a matter of fact, it actually happens more frequently with adult women!* I was dating a newly established entrepreneur. We met in a professional work setting, and he expressed his interest in getting to know me more personally. After exchanging contact information we began to date and enjoy each other's company frequently.

I was quickly drawn to his motivation, good looks, perseverance, and I began to daydream about the possible outcomes of our dating. *How often have you started planning your wedding after just one date with a man?* As my feelings led to relationship fantasies of being on his arm as his woman, I overlooked many red flags because I was married to false hope. *You know how we do.* I had already started thinking about the type of lifestyle I would have as his wife. I had thoughts about his proposal to me. I pictured the type of house we would have and the car we would drive. Girl, I convinced myself that I would be his woman, and he would treat me right!

Again, as I reflect, I now realize that I was actually more in love with his social status than him, and to be honest, I had no reason to be so infatuated with him because we were not even a couple! However, because I longed to have the relationships I saw in the media, and I wanted to be on the arm of a man who other women liked also, I deceived myself into believing our dates would turn me into his wife. I convinced myself to ignore his selfishness, pride, arrogance, insincerity, and yes - lack of transportation. I am ashamed to admit, that for many of our dates, I picked him up when I truly longed for a man to display chivalry toward me. Oh the things we do to experience the feelings of "love".

You see, this is what false hope will do! Because this is the chapter on false hope, you already know the outcome of this 'relationship' or lack thereof. Yes, he wined and dined me. Yes, he was in constant communication with me. Yes, I felt special while with him; however he never even initiated a committed relationship with me. Yet, there I was fantasizing about our future, and we had not *mentioned* marriage or even courtship! *Talk about FALSE HOPE!* Even worse, I had the audacity to be disappointed and let down as if *he* led me on, when I didn't get the happily ever after ending I dreamt of. *Silly, right?* Just as ridiculous as it sounds, is just as real the power false-hope has on women everywhere!

DO YOU HAVE FALSE-HOPE SYNDROME?

As I stated before, it is always easier to identify the issues in someone else's life, more than your own. I'm sure as you read my stories it was evident that I was dealing with false-hope syndrome.

Now - think about yourself. Have you been living with the symptoms of false hope? Are you currently committed to false hope? Are you ignoring his red flags while trying to force yourself into the title of his girl, woman, or wife, when in actuality it is clear that there is a slim chance of that taking place? Are you refusing to face the facts and reality?

Are you giving your all to someone, trying to prove to them that you are the one? This too is an indication of false hope syndrome. You are aspiring and anticipating more with him so desperately, that you stoop as low as to persuade him to be in agreement with you. Let me tell you, you do not want to do this. You want a man who will propose to you *without* your persuasion. You want a man who will be in a committed relationship with you without you having to beg, convince him, or prove yourself. Stop trying to influence him.

A real man knows what he wants and will eagerly go for it. Do you not realize that it is when you are committed to false hope that you appear desperate and a man can use you up very easily until you are empty? The reality is that men can recognize when a woman is living by false hope concerning him because he is the one that knows what his intentions are with you. Even though it is not fair to women, men will even allow you to demonstrate your love for them and let you convince them of your aspirations, only to leave you lonely in the end. *This* is why you must not live by false hope!

BREAK UP WITH FALSE HOPE

Until you break up with false hope, you will be left brokenhearted every time. You cannot live in a fantasy world any longer and you must know that you will not always have fairytale endings. As a coach, I have met so many women who all share the same dilemma. They are caught up in false hope! The most common stories entail women desiring to marry a man; however the man has expressed his hesitancy in pursuing marriage with them. Despite the man's verbal confession of his uncertainty and indecisiveness, the women insist they can 'win him over' or that with "a little space", he will recognize that she is the one for him. Very rarely, does this happen. My sister, if you are in this predicament, or if you know someone who is, *this may sting a bit,* but you/they need to be kicked out of your/their fantasy world!

A pattern I have noticed with women in this situation is that they have what I call *selective hearing & consideration.* What I mean is that they choose not to believe a man's words when they are unfavorable to their ears. Many women tend to believe a man without a shadow of a doubt if he says "I love you" even if he may be cheating, beating, and abusing them. Yet, if a man says, "I'm not ready for marriage" or "I need space" and "I'm not sure if I can see myself with you long term", women decide not to "hear" or "consider" *these* words. It's as if the man's words are falling onto deaf ears. Why? Because these women are living by false hope in a fantasy world. They are so desperate to make their vision and dream their reality that they choose not to believe the facts and instead allow their feelings to rule.

Is this you? Have you been, or are you one of these women right now? If so, first I commend you on recognizing this so that you can avoid living by false hope any longer. Secondly I want to encourage you to trust God OVER your feelings. Allow God to rule in your love life instead of letting your feelings control you. If your relationship with a man is not progressing in the way you hoped or dreamt, you must shift your mindset and know that this is perfectly okay! After all, why would you want to be with a man who is not completely into you? Moreover, you need to shift your mindset from being dissatisfied to being content because now you can actually start to position yourself for your true husband; the man God wants to send your way! You cannot be found by him, while in the chains of false hope or being wrapped up in the arms of your fantasy man. I want you to understand that God is preparing a special man, his *best* just for you, but you will not be emotionally, spiritually, or mentally ready for him if you continue to dwell in your dreams instead of getting in alignment with God's will for you! Forsake false hope from this day forward and put all of your hope, trust, and FAITH in God OVER your FEELINGS. It is not until you surrender your own plan, that you make room for God's will in your life. BREAK UP WITH FALSE HOPE!

Ready4TheRing Plan of Action:
Break Up With False Hope

- Take some time to journal and reflect upon your past relationships and experiences with dating. Identify the times when you were living by false hope. Write down your feelings about each relationship/man and what you hoped would have been. Then write down the facts about the situation and about the man. After about 2 days, review your notes and look for patterns in your relationships and your feelings.

- After reviewing your notes from action step 1, write down your patterns. Next ask God to empower and help you to break the cycle of false hope. Repent for trusting your feelings and your own plan over His will for your life. Commit to aligning your will to His.

- Make a commitment to God and yourself that you will wait patiently IN God's will for Him to send you your husband. Decide to allow a man to pursue you and that you will no longer compromise in an attempt to make your dreams a reality.

NOTES:

Chapter 6: Kiss The Past Goodbye

❖ *Jewel of Wisdom:*

In order to become ONE with your husband, you must let go of the past. You cannot be married to your future husband and the past at the same time. Kiss the past goodbye! #Ready4TheRing

So you are READY to be married? This is the chapter of the book that will partially test your marriage readiness. Marriage is not just about having a lifelong companion and having someone to make love to whenever you want without the feelings of conviction. Marriage is more than having a 'boo' to take pictures with to post on social media and see how many 'likes' and comments you get. Marriage is more than having a man to take care of you, a fancy wedding, and getting a big diamond ring on your finger. Marriage is a covenant, a promise between you, your spouse, and God. Below is just a portion of the promise you will make unto your husband and to God while at the altar.

You will vow to *"take this man to be your husband to live together after God's ordinance in the Holy Estate of matrimony in sickness and in health, and* ***forsaking*** *all others keep thee only unto him as long as you both shall live."*

You say you are ready for marriage, but are you truly *ready* to **forsake** all others?

According to the Merriam-Webster's Online Dictionary, to **forsake** is to: renounce or turn away from entirely. When you forsake something or someone, you give it up completely; you abandon, leave, and relinquish *it* or *them.*

When you marry your husband you are making a commitment to forsake all other men, **past**, **present**, and **future**, cleaving to your husband only. I know you have already had it in your mind that you are not supposed to entertain relationships with other men *after* you are married, but have you truly considered that you must forsake the men in your past? The truth of the matter is, you must also forsake men from your past *and* even men who you may have been dating up until you entered into courtship with your future husband. You will be making a commitment to leave and abandon them ALL.

So, do you *really* want to be married? If you still do, that's awesome! Now let me say this to you:

Simply SAYING "I Do" does not automatically change WHAT you do.

Many women and even men are deceived into believing that as soon as they get married, habits that they had as a single individual will automatically change because they are in a marital commitment. This could not be further from the truth. This is why, preparation before marriage is essential. You must begin to transform your habits, lifestyle, connections, and mindset prior to marriage; and starting *before* engagement and a committed relationship is even better! You need to start now!

THE TEST: FORSAKING ALL OTHERS

The privilege of cleaving to your husband sounds so appealing, and that love experience is what I am sure you are longing for. We all desire an unbreakable connection with someone special. I'm sure after your last break up you've made a resolution in your mind to leave that man alone because he hurt you and you just needed to move on. While this decision is great, it is time to consider whether you have *actually* left him and every other man you were once with alone. Have you forsaken them completely?

I speak to women all the time who claim that they are 'over' their exes and that they have moved forward, leaving them behind. As I ask them questions to confirm this is true, I often find that these same women are caught in a mental illusion. They believe they have moved forward, leaving their ex in the past; however, the truth is that they have not done so entirely. Are you caught in this same mental illusion?

Think about at least the last 2 men you were in a relationship with and answer the following self-evaluation questions honestly. Get a small piece of paper and write down a simple *yes* or *no.*

- Do I still have his phone number saved in my phone?

- Do I still have text message threads from our conversations stored in my phone?

- Do I have voice messages lingering in the voice mail inbox on my phone?

- The last time he called me since our break up, did I answer the phone?

- Have I called him since our relationship has ended?

- Have I deleted all pictures of him and of us from my phone?

- Am I still friends with him on Facebook?

- Have I deleted any personal Facebook messages which were shared between us before and during our relationship?

- Have I <u>blocked</u> his Facebook account completely so I cannot see his profile and he cannot see mine at all?

- Have I disposed of all gifts, pictures, and possessions in my house, room, car, at my job, etc. that remind me of him, that he left, or that he gave me?

- Have I deleted and/or blocked him on Twitter, Instagram, and all other social media sites in which we were connected?

- Do I (Will I) <u>refuse</u> to see him and/or go out with him even if he apologizes and treats me nicely to make up for the heartache and breakup?

I know I've listed a number of questions for you to answer honestly and I sure hope you did. The truth is, if you cannot kiss the past goodbye you will not be able to become ONE with your future husband while still being connected with men from your past. I strongly encourage you to delete, block, dispose, and actively rid yourself from all things that will keep his image and/or likeness in your thoughts, mind, and in your sight both physically and virtually. Actively engaging in doing so, may sound extreme to you, but disconnecting yourself with previous men completely is the true essence of *forsaking all others*.

Now, you may be thinking that these steps are unnecessary right now because you are not married. This is untrue. Remember I told you, *saying "I Do" does not change what you do*. This means, if you are spying on his Facebook profile now, trying to see what he's doing, whether or not he's talking about you, or if his new girl looks better than you - then guess what? Being married will not change this! You will continue to secretly stalk his page and keep up with his life on Instagram, etc. While married, you will *still* be tempted to call him and to possibly meet up with him because the enemy of your soul knows your weaknesses and he is seeking if he may devour you and your marriage. *Yes, honey, the enemy is that real!*

I don't mean to harp on Facebook, but as popular as it is, you must know that there are statistics which show that Facebook has been listed as a common cause for divorce amongst couples. According to a Huffington

Post online article published in 2013, Russell Clayton, a doctoral student in the University of Missouri School of Journalism, conducted research and found that "excessive Facebook users are more likely to connect or reconnect with other Facebook users, including previous partners, which may lead to emotional and physical cheating." Clayton told Huffington Post Divorce via e-mail that "high levels of Facebook use is associated with negative relationship outcomes for newer couples (three years or less)." [2]

This is not to say that Facebook is a negative social media tool; however without proper monitoring and usage, it can become easy for you to remain in contact or reconnect with your exes. This should not happen once you are married, and the way to ensure this is to sever all ties before you even meet your future husband.

In fact, if you still are in contact in any fashion with someone from your past, your chances of even being married may be at risk. Why? Because when you are focused on your past and keeping in touch with previous partners in any manner, you are not allowing yourself to be in a proper mental, emotional, spiritual, or physical position to be found. When you entertain thoughts about your ex, when you try to be friends with him after the break up, when you keep relationship paraphernalia, you prohibit yourself from being mentally and emotionally available to a man who may be interested in you. This is how you miss out on a 'good man'; by being occupied with the counterfeit! Many times, the counterfeit is not just someone new; it is likely that it is a man from your past! You need to LET HIM GO! FORSAKE HIM!

DATING HIM WHILE FLIRTING WITH THE PAST

Before my husband and I were engaged, we courted for about 6 months seriously because we believed God was leading our relationship toward marriage. During this time, we discovered our likes, dislikes, similarities, differences, and perspectives on various topics such as religion, the workplace, family, music, media, politics, and relationships. Within the relationship conversations, my then boyfriend, now husband, Julian, would ask me how I knew that I was ready for a marital commitment. He would ask what I had done in my season of singleness to prepare myself for the future. Such a loaded question! I had never had anyone ask me such thought provoking, serious questions until I started dating him.

In response to his questions about what I had done to prepare myself, I shared with him that I had read a few marriage prep books, I read the bible and know scriptures about marriage, I surrendered my will to God, and have allowed Him to transform my life and renew me before meeting my husband. That was a big step for me, because for many years I was living contrary to the Word of God, especially while in college, and particularly when it came to my relationships with men. By this point in our relationship, I had already shared with Julian about my previous relationships, including my sexual history, and his response to me was, "How do you know that you are over the men you have had sex with?" *Ouch!* I had never thought someone would ask me a question such as this. I believed in my heart that I was 'over' them. After all, I was left heartbroken and empty after my experiences with them. Additionally, I thought I didn't need to *get over* some of the guys I dated because I did not have a true connection with them in the first place.

When he asked me about being over the men I had sex with, quite honestly I was offended. I *knew* I had moved past them and I wanted nothing to do with them. For goodness sake, I cried out to the Lord like David and asked God to *create in me a clean heart, and renew a right spirit within me!* I denounced and renounced the spirits I became one with and said prayers to break spiritual soul ties. I confessed my sin and asked God to forgive me and cleanse me! I didn't renounce spirits and repent to God to still be connected with those men! I had been to the altar several times and had prayer warriors pray over me. Certainly, I had forsaken them. Yes, I was over them! I hadn't even spoken to many of them in years! How dare he ask me how I knew if I was indeed over my exes? Why didn't he have confidence and trust in the transformational and renewing work that God had done within me! I believed God cleansed me. I believed he made me whole. I believed that my repentance and renewal would serve as enough evidence of me moving pass the past; why would he even ask me that?

After I shared my evidence with him verbally, he politely asked me, "So you're not friends with any of them on Facebook right?....I'm sure you don't keep in contact with them." *WHOA!* At that very moment, my heart dropped into my stomach, my mouth became as dry as sand paper, and I was as nervous as a guilty person on the stand of the courtroom. I couldn't lie. We were building our relationship on trust. How was I going to tell him that I *was* still friends with them? I sat there on the couch in shock. What was I going to do? Honestly, I had never given thought to deleting them on Facebook, and I actually did still have many of their numbers in my phone. It had not occurred to me that this was a problem. I finally gained the courage to say, "Yes, I'm still friends with them on Facebook, and yes, I still have their numbers in my phone." Just as stunned as I was when he asked me how I knew that I was over them, was just as astonished as he was finding out that I was still connected with them! His face was overcome with disappointment and concern. He expressed that he could not understand how I could have been delivered, restored, and renewed from impurity and my past, but yet still remain connected with the very people I was cleansed and set free from! After attempting to explain that *it wasn't a big deal*, conviction pierced my soul like a bolt of lightning! I had tried to defend myself, but everything I said only made me sound foolish and naïve. *How could I be moving forward in a committed relationship with a man whom I love, and who loves me completely and still have connections, see pictures, exchange words with, and even have the phone numbers of people who I once was physically involved with?*

SEVERING THE TIES: ESTABLISHING TRUST

At the start of the chapter, I asked you to reflect on several questions. Do you see why now? Many times as women, we are so naïve in our thinking that almost anything goes at times! Like you, I had not thought that doing a clean sweep of my Facebook account (that was the only social network I was a part of at the time) was essential to securing the restoring work that Jesus did within my heart and soul. The question had now become was I *really* renewed? After much prayer and soul-searching, I realized God had indeed completed his work within me spiritually, but I had to 'walk out' my deliverance and do my part in the natural realm, which needed to be in alignment with his internal cleansing within me. I realized that yes, I needed to sever all connections, regardless of how subtle. The truth was, I had not had conversation with these guys in years, and

I barely saw their profiles in my news feed. They really were not active persons in my life.

The truth was, their numbers were not on my speed dial, nor had I talked to them on the phone since our involvement. The truth was, I was no longer keeping up with them, and our relationship was over so *there was no* need to have their contacts via phone or internet. As I continued my soul search, I realized I had pictures of them and/or us on my computer which needed to go also. The real truth was, while I allowed men from my past to still occupy unrented space in my life, I could not expect to move forward with who I believed God sent as my husband. Pictures, numbers, and connections with guys from my past still lingering in my life had to go. Since Julian asked me about my connection with them, refusing to sever the ties would do nothing but cause him to question my commitment and seriousness in moving toward marriage with him.

The next day, Julian and I had a meeting with my laptop. We went through my Facebook profile and I hit the button to 'unfriend' all the men from my past. Then, I went into my personal settings and blocked them! I deleted pictures from my computer. I deleted numbers from my phone. I did it! Whewww! It was at that moment that I truly kissed my past goodbye! In that very same moment, I knew it was the beginning of *forsaking all others*. Julian wanted to marry me, and I was committed to building our relationship on trust. To this day, those people are still blocked and I am happily married without any emotional or physical Facebook affairs!

WE BROKE UP, BUT WE'RE STILL "FRIENDS"

Do you still have conversations with your ex? Do the two of you hang out occasionally or keep each other company when you're 'bored'? Do you grab a bite to eat, go see a movie, or watch each other's children? Do you go to family functions together, church, or other public events? Are you still having sex as if you are a married couple? If this does not describe you personally, that's great, but I am sure you have a sister-girl who it does describe! Everyone knows they broke up months ago, yet you would almost question whether they truly did, because they are still inseparable.

If this is you, I urge you to stop! If you know someone in this situation, encourage them to break this cycle! Remaining 'friends' with a guy after the relationship has ended is not healthy. In actuality, it is likely that you are still emotionally connected and if you had sex, there is definitely a bond (soul tie) that exists, which is why you or your friend is having such a difficult time kissing the past goodbye!

Here's the deal, when you remain in contact with your ex, and when you are out with them in public, why *would* another man want to approach you even if he was interested in you? You look like you are 'taken' and unavailable. I know there are *some* men out there who will approach you even with a ring on your finger, but a true man of God would not approach you if it appears you are involved with another man. Please realize that continuing the relationship with your ex without an official title is not helping you prepare for marriage or position yourself to be found. Moreover, continuing to be with him is an indicator that you are not truly over him either. If you insist that you have moved past him, but you are still going out with him, then I encourage you to check your motives.

If you are with him so that you can pass the time without being lonely, or you want a free meal and movie, then what does this say about you? What character trait are you demonstrating? I would have to say selfishness, and this is not a good trait to exude if you desire to be married. However, there is hope! You can decide today to no longer entertain previous partners. You can decide today to move pass your past! You can decide today, to end the "friendship" so that both of you can be free and redirect your energy on God's will for your life. If you all have broken up, it may be safe to say that you realized being with him was not God's will for you at all. Moreover, as I mentioned in Chapter 1, you need time to heal and refocus after a breakup no matter how severe or light. You owe it to yourself. Lastly, your future husband will appreciate your initiative to kiss your past goodbye instead of being friends with your ex while trying to build a marriage with him.

RELFECTION TIME

Just like with every other chapter you have read in the book thus far, I speak on issues that I have faced and I know many single women do too. I am sharing all the content in this book with you while you are single so you know what to do now in order to prepare yourself for marriage, and so you know what it takes to position yourself as a wife. I started this chapter by asking you are you *really ready for marriage?* Though there is much more to the wedding vows, **forsaking** all others is a HUGE commitment. When I made the decision on my part to forsake the men in my past, my mind was focused on Christ and the husband I believed he sent me. Just 1-2 years earlier, I would not have even entertained the idea of doing a phone and social media clean sweep! I would have looked the man I was with at the time in the eye and said, "You're crazy to think I'm doing all of that for you!" My point in sharing this with you is that, back then, I was all about *Teresa.* I was selfish. I was not forsaking anything or anyone unless I wanted to. If I did not think the slight connections I had with men were a distraction for me, then I would not have deleted them.

Here's a moment of truth, if you have been reading this chapter and you have been thinking to yourself "*I would not have done all of that*", "*She's crazy*" or "*I'm over my past, but I don't need to go to that extreme*" then sis, I have news for you - it is likely that you are not ready for marriage! You see, preparation for marriage goes beyond your decisions, but it begins with your mindset and your heart. My prayer is that as you have been reading this chapter, you have allowed God to soften your heart and speak to you of the importance of kissing your past goodbye so you can be in position to receive God's best. If I would not have deleted and cleansed my life of my past relationship partners, I would not be married today. I know this, because my husband told me; and I knew this deep in my heart. My sister, it is impossible to be married to your future husband while remaining connected to your past. Leave the past behind. Take the literal, physical action steps to demonstrate it. Now it is *your turn* to kiss the past goodbye!

Ready4TheRing Plan of Action
Kiss The Past Goodbye!

- Go back and read each question I asked you to reflect on at the beginning of the chapter and answer them thoroughly on a piece of paper. Answer the questions, thinking about all the men you have dated, been in committed relationships with, and who you were sexually involved with in any way.

- Delete all the phone numbers of men you were involved with in the past.

- "Unfriend", delete, block, and unfollow all of the men you were involved with from all of your social media networks.

- Dispose of all gifts, pictures, and possessions in your house, room, car, at your job, etc. that remind you of him, that he left, or that he gave you.

- Cease all communication with men who you have been involved with in the past (does not include the father of your children if applicable). End the 'friendships' you have with any of your exes.

- Ask God to cleanse and purify you of the past relationships you have had. Ask him to reveal to you other areas of your past which you need to kiss goodbye!

NOTES:

Chapter 7: Stick To Your Standards

❖ *Jewel of Wisdom:*

Having standards will allow you to experience a caliber of man that is more in alignment with your true desire. When you lower your standards, you make yourself vulnerable to regret, disappointment, and frustration due to your own decision to compromise. It is time to break the cycle of compromise, and stick to your standards! #Ready4TheRing

He was tall, dark, handsome, and every time he spoke, he made me melt like chocolate under a hot summer sun. He knew just the right compliments to offer each time I saw him. He always called my phone at the perfect moment; and he was there to lift me up when I had a rough day. He was sweet, thoughtful, funny, and kind. It had been a long time since someone made me feel this good.

I did not want to give this feeling up; I wanted this to continue! Who wouldn't have? So I continued to date him, hoping that the two of us could have a long-lasting relationship even though he could not keep a job, he did not have a car, he was camping out at a friend's house for free, he had abusive tendencies, a sexual addiction, and a history of unfaithfulness. The "perk" was that he was a Christian man. He was actively involved in church and no one knew how he *really* was. I believed for sure that he would change. Even though he had not been a faithful man prior to me, I honestly thought by him being with *me* that I could change him. Even though I had earned my bachelors' and master's degrees and he had not finished undergraduate school, nor did he have a full time job, I chose to think optimistically by believing that eventually he would make a decent living. Yes, he was emotionally & verbally abusive at times, and even gripped me up a time or two; however, his words like honey soothed my concerns and nervousness every time. He showed me he liked me, he said he loved me, and I was determined to believe him. Why not give him a chance? In the past, I dated men who appeared to have their life more in order than he did, but the relationship did not work out. Why not try something new? I anticipated spending time with him because out of the many other women he could have chosen, I caught his eye. Yes, I will give this a try!

Have you ever met a guy that just blew you away and swept you off of your feet? Good looking, made you feel loved, lavished you with gifts, compliments, attention, and more? He was always there when you needed company, he made you smile, kept you daydreaming, and he met your emotional needs? Yes, he may have had a *few* flaws; well maybe more like many, but you were willing to overlook them because you loved the way he made you feel? He may have owned a pinto or lemon instead of a Mercedes. He may have even had some unattractive habits such as using profanity, spending more money on material items than investing in his future, being prideful, arrogant, or selfish at times? He may not have been fully dedicated to his own success and mooched off of others? Quite possibly, he had multiple children with a different baby-mama but you were willing to overlook that misfortune too? Maybe his criminal background was less than perfect or his status was something other than single; like dating another woman, engaged to his fiancé, or married. Although he warmed the pew at church from time to time, he may have been biblically illiterate and spiritually empty, BUT you *still* wanted to be with him? In spite of all the flaws, he just had a way of tapping into your feelings and you were going to give this man a chance, thinking *"Forget about what I used to want, maybe this man here could provide it and more!"*

Am I talking to you? Girl, I have been in situations just like this, right along with you! At some point in our lives, we both decided to *"see the best in him"* and as much as we may not want to admit it, we believed we had Superwoman powers, which would set him free from his flaws for him to become the man we **truly** wanted! We hoped that he would turn out to be a Christian. We hoped he would overcome the random fits of anger. We hoped he would become financially stable. We hoped he would rid himself of ungodly habits. We even hoped he would leave his girlfriend or wife. We hoped *we* would be the lucky woman, even if that meant we would lay down our standards for a chance of him kneeling down on one knee with a ring. Truth is, in hindsight, we **abandoned** our standards against our better judgment, ignored the conviction, and decided to COMPROMISE. *Ouch! (I know the truth hurts sometimes)* What happened is: we saw his POTENTIAL and we believed that certainly, one day he would walk in that potential fully and we would then be the happiest woman on earth!

THE IMPORTANCE OF STANDARDS

Too often as women, we are too quick to compromise our standards in exchange for a man's care, kindness, kiss, and commitment. We excuse and overlook what he does not have or who he *really* is just so we can have a man, even if he is not the man we believe God would send as His perfect and **best gift** for us.

According to the "Hunt" Dictionary, (*my definition),* **Compromise** is to accept into your life, and give opportunity to a man who does not meet your standards but meets your emotional needs; therefore you pray that his *presence* IN your life is God's *plan* FOR your life.

I cannot believe how many times I was guilty of this offense before I was married! If you fit in this boat with me, let me tell you - it is time for you to make this a habit of the past. You cannot do this anymore. Stop lowering your standards. Do not adjust what you desire in a man for a counterfeit man that does not come even close! Honey, STICK TO YOUR STANDARDS!

The "Hunt" Dictionary defines **Standards** as " A measure, level, or a set of expectations that align with your authentic desires which a man must match **before** allowing him access to your time and a place in your heart."

Standards are designed to help you decipher which men you should allow into your space, and which men you should dismiss.

Catch this! Not every man who **approaches** you needs to have **ACCESS** to you! Not every man who expresses interest IN you has your best interest IN MIND.

Sis, your standards are supposed to weed-out the men who do not align with your morals, values, perspective, desires, beliefs, *and* your religious views! (that's right sis, you should not be involved with a man who does not worship the same God that you serve).

Having standards does not limit your opportunity to experiencing true love. Instead, standards increase your likelihood of experiencing true love with the *right* person.

When you compromise by allowing a man into your life who is not in alignment with what you desire for yourself, you will never experience the fulfillment you wish to have. Why? Because you are expecting a man who is not what you truly want to *become* someone that he is not! That is like expecting a grape to become a banana! If you want a banana, you need to get a banana and not a grape. So I say to you - if you want a man who is faithful, do not date a man who you know is a playboy. If you want a man who is going to love you like Christ loves the church, then do not allow yourself to become infatuated with a man who only attends "Bed-side Baptist".

If you want a man who will marry you without your persuasion, then do not get involved with a man who is already committed to another woman. If you want a man who demonstrates chivalry, then do not date a man who lacks proper manners. I know this sounds extremely obvious and simple, but sometimes our common sense dissipates when we want a committed relationship, and *we want it now! Frequently* lowering your standards is a result of your lack of faith in God. If God is able to do exceedingly, abundantly above all we ask of him or think, then why do you not trust that God will exceed what you even think you need in a man? God wants to bless you with His best! Stop settling for less in order to experience a false representation of "love". You need to trust that in God's timing, He will send you a man that will do more than meet your standards, but exceed your expectations! It is your faith in Him that will cause you to forsake compromising at any time! It is time to stick to your standards!

LET ME CLARIFY... DON'T GET IT TWISTED

Now, I am not saying to have a long list of standards and "must-haves" for a man that you don't even match. Nor am I suggesting that you will come in contact with a "perfect" man who has no flaws at all. I also do not want to give you the impression that the husband God has for you will indeed meet *your* every "requirement". I AM SAYING however, to stop eradicating your standards because you have become weary in your waiting on God to bless you with His best. **Do not**

minimize your expectations of a man, just because he sooths your emotions. More importantly, you cannot afford to neglect biblical principles and your moral values in order to become a bride or be married soon. I know at times it may not appear to be so, but there *are* STILL good men out there! There are high-quality men around who are not taken! You do not have to "accept" just "any ole thing"!

When you have standards, men know that they cannot approach you and/or treat you carelessly. **You** set the tone of a man's interaction and relationship with you based on what you accept and allow. This is why you must know what you stand for. The old adage is true, *If you don't stand for something, you'll fall for anything"*. Listen, if you do not have some form of standards, you will fall for anything and anyone. Moreover, if you disregard or lower your standards you are only cheating yourself and setting yourself up for disappointment. It is important to note that a man, who truly likes you and has interest in you, will rise to your standards; whereas, a man who does not have your best interest in mind will be turned off and will run from your standards. (And this is what you want!) Time is something you cannot rewind or get back, so you cannot afford to waste yours. If a man is not serious about you and does not match your standards, let him go on his merry way. You don't have time to waste, nor do you have time to be preoccupied with a man who is not serious about looking for his wife when you desire to be married.

ESTABLISHING STANDARDS

After writing his book *Act Like a Lady, Think Like a Man,* Steve Harvey shared *this* while talking about women and standards during an interview with Oprah, "You've got sports fishermen, and you've got guys out there fishing to eat. You've got guys that are fishing to keep the fish, and you've got guys that are fishing to catch them, unhook them and throw them back," ...."You've got to determine along the way which one of the fish you're going to be."[1]

Without ironclad standards, Steve says you will always end up back in the dating pool. "**You've got to quit lowering your standards**"...."**Set your requirements up front so when a guy hooks you, he has to know this is business.**"

Did you get the message? You have got to have standards in place that let a man know that <u>you mean business</u>. He needs to understand that you are not tolerating mediocrity in his interactions with you. Remember, I told you earlier in the chapter that YOU set the tone for the relationships by what you accept and what you allow. So the question you need to ask yourself is, "What will I accept?" and "What will I allow?" The answer to these questions should range from the initial starting point of *What will I accept when a man approaches me* to *What will I accept throughout the duration of our potential relationship?* The same thing goes for the question "What will I allow?" *What will allow when he is getting to know me? What will be allowed while we are in a relationship?*

You MUST have your personal standards identified BEFORE you even meet a man. If not, you will waiver in your standards and develop them as you go along. This can be harmful considering a woman's feelings and emotions are fickle and deceiving. Once you become emotionally involved with a man, it will be more difficult to effectively uphold the standards you desire. They need to be established NOW.

You know at the end of the chapter I will give you an action plan! I am going to help you get started with one of the action steps now, so you have a clear understanding of what you need to do.

Let's start with the standards by defining question #1.
What will I accept when a man approaches me?

You need to think about the many ways guys have approached you. What did you like? What turned you off? As you reflect back, did the way a man approached you tell you more about his character? *Most likely so!* Now identify the type of approach that is acceptable to you? What should his body language suggest? What type of speech is attractive to you? Is there a certain demeanor and dress code that is important to you? Do you have a preference about whether he approaches you alone or with a group of people? You need to give consideration to all of these measures. These and more, mark the foundation of what you deem as acceptable or unacceptable. And yes, it is perfectly okay not to accept just 'any ole thing'.

As an example, I'll share what was acceptable to me in relation to a man's approach. These were standards I established for myself after years of not realizing their importance. That is why I found myself disappointed and frustrated many times before I met my husband, because I did not stand for something. (Just like you, I thought I had standards, but many times I let them go by the wayside.)

MY EXAMPLE: **What will I accept when a man approaches me?**

- ✓ **My Standard:** He must be respectful in his approach and use language like "excuse me", "Hello, my name is________", "may I talk to you for a minute", etc. **instead** of *"Hey Ma" or "Yo, pretty lady" or "You is fine, let me get yo digits!"*

- I've heard these pick-up lines before, and I just was not going to accept this! *Excuse me sir....you sound crazy!* I was a professional woman and I needed to be approached as such. More importantly, I only wanted to allow people into my emotional space who were respectful. If a man approaches me with "Hey Ma!" then I know we do not share the same ideal about respect and this would be an issue in the future. *Yes! Something that appears to be so minute as an approach, in the big scheme of things does truly give you perspective of a person's character!*

✓ **My Standard:** His body language should be one of good posture and stature because this exudes confidence. I desired his head be held high, and that he make eye contact with me as he is talking. I wanted him to be respectful of my space, by not touching me (except through a mutually agreed upon handshake). He should not have his hand in his pants, or try to put his arm around me, etc.

- Eye contact is a way to measure a man's sincerity and good posture helps me determine his level of confidence and care for his own self. I did not want a man to touch me during his approach...*Excuse me sir...I don't know you like that!*

✓ **My Standard:** He must look presentable with properly fitted clothes, not sagging pants, nor jeans as tight as what a girl might wear either!

If we were in church, I prefer a man who wears his "Sunday Best" and not a flannel shirt with Timberland boots. If he's wearing a hat, I wanted him to know the importance of taking his hat off if approaching me inside of a building.

- As a woman who takes pride in her appearance, I desire a man who does as well. As an adult, long gone are the days when oversized, sagging clothes and a fitted hat are attractive. I wanted a man who had the appearance of maturity and self-care. *And sir....if your pants or shirt are tighter than mine - I may not be the woman for you!*

Those are just examples of the standards I set as it relates to a man's approach to me. First impressions are lasting impressions, and they give you a perception of an individual. Your standards also let a man know a little about you. If he can approach you recklessly and you accept his approach, then he knows he does not have to try very hard to impress you and he may possibly believe you are "*easy*". However, if your demeanor exudes that you do not accept nonsense, and a man knows he needs to approach you with respect, then you have now earned his! You want him to respect and honor you. Once he knows he can 'get over' on you without much 'work', the sooner he will try to get you *under him* without a commitment and you *know* what I mean! So again I say to you, establish your standards in this area! The sooner you can identify whether or not a man deserves to have access to you, the better you will be and the less time you will waste!

I don't want to overwhelm you with things to ponder, but I am compelling you to truly establish your standards! Many of the problems we experience in relationships are because we did not prohibit or prevent certain things. We compromised our standards, accepting and allowing more than what we should have. Then we place all the blame on the man. No ma'am, let's make sure we have required much before we relinquish our hearts, bodies, and emotions. We have to do better in the area of upholding our standards!

In an effort not to make the chapter too long, I will give a brief list of a few standards I had regarding the question ***What will I allow while we are in a relationship?*** This question is more so about *how you will allow a man to treat you. This reflects what you "stand for" and the expectations a man must meet. A man must uphold your standards for how you want to be treated. If they do not, then you do not need to continue to allow that man access to your time, or into your life, space, and emotions.*

- ✓ I will allow a man to speak to me with uplifting, positive, and encouraging words only. I will not accept a man's foul language, demeaning speech patterns toward me, or allow a man to be verbally abusive.

✓ I will allow a man to have physical contact (holding hands, etc.) with me with my approval and consent only. The moment a man is forceful or persistent with his contact, I will dismiss him from my life.

✓ I will allow a man to pursue me and exhibit leadership only and not passive behaviors. I do not want a man that I will have to lead or one that I can walk all over. I desire a mentally and spiritually strong man of God. I will allow a man to express his interest in me by calling me, picking *me* up to take me on dates, buying *me* gifts (if he desires), asking to meet my family, and more! If a man is not taking initiative to demonstrate his interest in me, I will not try to 'win him over' and persuade him that I am a good woman. I will not allow a man to be lazy in his pursuit and expression of interest in me. If he is, he is not the one for me.

You see, standards are for men, but standards are for YOU as well! When you are fully aware of what you want, what you will allow, and what you will accept, then any man who does not align with your desires will need to 'keep it steppin". In the first part of the book we talked about the importance of knowing who you are and understanding your true worth! When you know your worth, you will not accept someone or something that does not complement your worth!

The standards you set for yourself portray how you perceive your own worth. If a man believes that you are valuable, but your lack of standards will tell him otherwise, he will not work hard in pursuing you. Why? Because he had no need to! You did not require it of him? On the contrary, if a man believes you are priceless and he values you, plus your standards are in alignment with your worth, then that man will rise to the requirements you set because he wants to be with you!

YOU determine how a man will treat you!

YOUR standards determine how a man will perceive you!

YOUR ability to uphold your standards lets a man know how you value *yourself!*

Just as much as you are observing him, he is observing you! Demonstrate your respect and value for yourself by having high standards. A man who knows your worth and wants to make you his wife, will rise to your requirements! You will not have to compromise at all!

ARE MY STANDARDS TOO HIGH?

I have heard women say that their friends have told them their standards are too high. I personally do not believe that one's standards can be too high. I do believe that if you have been accused of having standards that are too high, then you should consider the following:

- There is a difference between having high standards and being downright shallow.

For example, if a man is actively pursuing you, he is a man of good character, he is spiritually mature, he is financially stable, but he drives a 1999 Oldsmobile instead of a 2015 Cadillac, and you do not want him to pick you up in his car, I would not say your standards are too high, I would say you have a shallow expectation.

- There is a difference between high standards and having unrealistic expectations.

If you want a man to say all the 'right' things at the 'right time', be a mind reader and know he was supposed to call you every 2 hours, take you to work, pick you up from work, help you take care of your kids, assist with some of your bills, wear high quality brands of clothes and shoes only, go everywhere you ask him to go, help with projects you are working on, give you money, be at your service, and do whatever you ask -

then my friend, it is not that your standards are high - you are just expecting way too much!

- There is a difference between having high standards, and *you* having lost your sensitivity to a man's expectations & perspective.

I see this all the time! If you expect a man to express his interest in you with respect, admiration, love, honor, and esteem; but you talk to him with sarcasm, continue to point out his flaws and nag him, constantly complain even when he's doing his best, you bash him on social media, and embarrass him in front of your/his friends with your dishonoring speech and privileged/bouji disposition, then sis, you have lost your mind! I don't mean to be offensive, but if you do all this, you have completely offended and disrespected your mate. You cannot expect his admiration unto you, when you do not admire him in the same.

So, if someone has told you that you need to lower your standards, or that your standards are too high, may I suggest to you that you may need to eliminate your shallowness, unrealistic expectations, or your insensitivity to manhood.

Your friends are probably saying this to you because they know you will not get a man if you keep this up! And honey, you won't! So I encourage you to re-evaluate yourself before you require anything else from a man. Keep in mind that you should not require from someone else what you do not meet yourself. Also know that there is a thin line between having standards and being picky & obsessive with particulars.

NON-NEGOTIABLES

One last thing before we end this chapter. Non-negotiable standards are just that: non-negotiable. No matter what, you absolutely will not budge or accept what is not in alignment with this standard. Standards are meant to be followed and adhered to, but I understand that sometimes, depending on the circumstance, you may ease up or bend slightly. There is no wiggle room with Non-Negotiables however.

As a Christian, your first Non-Negotiable should be:

ANY MAN YOU DATE **MUST** BE A CHRISTIAN!!!!

You cannot bend on this! You should not waiver on this! The bible is very clear about being equally yoked.

Another Non-Negotiable should be:

HE **MUST NOT** BE MARRIED OR CURRENTLY INVOLVED IN A RELATIONSHIP.

If he is married, he is off-limits! It does not matter if he is separated. It does not matter if he and his wife live in separate houses, or in different states. HE IS *STILL MARRIED!* How can you dishonor another woman's marriage by being in relationship with her husband, and then expect that God will honor your marriage to him? How can you expect other women to honor your future marriage when in the past you did not honor others'? What comes around goes around. Every seed has a season of harvest. Be careful. Do not do this. It will come back to you!

A third Non-Negotiable ought to be:

HE **MUST BE COMMITTED** TO FOLLOWING CHRIST'S LORDSHIP OVER HIS LIFE.

There is a difference between one simply saying they are a Christian versus a man submitted and yielding his own will in order to be obedient to God's will for his life. This is why it is important to have discussions about his and your relationships with the Lord before entering into a committed relationship. You must remember that the bible says for husbands to love their wives as Christ loves the church and for wives to submit to their husbands as unto the Lord. This means, if you were to marry the man who has interest in you, you will have to allow him to lead, and you submit. This will be a very difficult task if the man is not following after God and allowing God to lead him. You must not date allowing God to lead him. You must not date haphazardly and have aimless conversations when getting to know a man. You must be very intentional.

These are the top 3 Non-Negotiable Standards I recommend all Christian women implement. There are more to add to the list, and I certainly welcome you to do so. Remember, Non-Negotiable Standards are expectations and requirements that a man must absolutely meet before you allow him into your life and emotional space.

WHAT DOES THIS HAVE TO DO WITH MARRIAGE?

Men marry women they value! Your standards speak highly of your self-perceived value. If you require that a man meet your standards before you allow them access and continued access into your life, you validate that you are a woman of worth. On the other hand, if you do not have standards, or you disregard them and compromise, not requiring that a man 'come correct', you show him that you devalue your worth. Why should he value you more than you value yourself?

Men respect women with standards. Men will rise to the standards you set if they believe you are the wife for them!

If you compromise, you will allow yourself to be in a relationship which is not completely fulfilling just to experience the sentiments of love. Not only will you end up frustrated because you are dating a man's POTENTIAL instead of his true PERSON, but you will not be in POSITION to be found by, nor to receive into your life the TRUE man God is preparing for you.

I say to you, stop settling, do not compromise, and stick to your standards. Trust that God is preparing a man who will meet and exceed your standards. More importantly, use the Word of God to develop your standards. God is not going to send you a man who is not in alignment with Him or His Word. This will help you recognize both God's best gift for you and help you not to be distracted by the men who are not God's gift to you.

Ready4TheRing Plan Of Action:
Establish Your Standards & Stick To Them

- ❖ Take a moment to reflect on the times when you compromised your standards in order to experience feelings of love and admiration. Once you've identified these times, pray and ask God to forgive you for not trusting Him enough to wait for Him to send you a man that you would not have to compromise for.

- ❖ It's time to establish your standards. Identify what you will allow and what you will accept. Answer the following questions (you may look back in the chapter as a guide.) List each question in your journal and answer each question after careful thought and consideration.

1. What will I accept when a man is approaching me?

2. What will I accept throughout the duration of our potential relationship?

3. What will allow when a man is getting to know me?

4. What will be allowed while we are in a relationship?

- Define your "Non-Negotiables". These are requirements and expectations that are deal-makers or deal-breakers. Above everything else you've listed, these Non-Negotiables have got to be in alignment with God's Word. These are your "must" statements, which you will not renege on under no circumstance. A man MUST meet these or else he will absolutely not have a chance of relationship with you.

- Ask God to help you commit to upholding your standards. An example prayer would be:

Dear Lord, I trust and believe that you are preparing a special man for me. I believe that he will be just what I need, and he will even exceed what I think I want and require. I pray that you will empower me to uphold the standards I have set for myself and men who are interested in me. I know that because these standards are in accordance with your will, that they will help me recognize whether or not the man who is interested in me is sent from you or sent as a distraction. Lord, I need your help to discern the difference, and I ask that you will help me to uphold these standards and not compromise. In Jesus' name I pray, Amen.

NOTES:

Chapter 8:
No More Sleeping Evangelist

❖ *Jewel of Wisdom:*

You must decide which woman you will be: A woman of honor or a woman of hypocrisy. If it is a woman of honor, you must be a godly example <u>before</u> him instead of being a booty call lying <u>underneath</u> him. If you want to stand out as a 'good' thing who is a woman of integrity, do not be the typical 'church girl'. No more Sleeping Evangelist for you! Rise above the spirit of sexual immorality and hypocrisy and be the woman of honor God has purposed you to be! *<u>#Ready4TheRing</u>*

It happens all the time. She is a singer. She is an usher. She is the armor bearer to the First Lady. She directs the choir. She teaches Sunday School or Bible Study. She reads the scripture. She sits in the pulpit. She preaches. She teaches. She lays hands and prophesies. She is the epitome of a woman of God committed to Christ. She does all the right things in church. She waves her hands and shouts "Hallelujah!" She claps her hands and sways with the choir. She will even cut a fancy step with 4 inch heels during the praise break, and she may even run a lap around the church. She appears to have it all together and while the onlookers wonder why she is not married yet, the church mothers dare to ask the question, "Honey, when you get'tin mar'ried?"

She smiles back at Mother and says, "I'm waiting on the Lord, whenever He sees fit to send my Boaz, then I'll be married". She leaves the conversation, disguising her disgust because she has been wondering the very same thing. What she does not realize is that she cannot experience the fullness of her desires, while at the same time prohibiting her very desire from becoming reality. She is oblivious to the fact that while she thinks she is preparing herself for marriage, she is prohibiting her ability to position herself as a 'good thing' because she continues to position herself in a bed with a man. She thinks she is spiritually mature; however she has not fully surrendered her premarital sexual desires to the Lord. Her invisible bonds with past and present sexual partners have kept her enslaved to repeating the cycle of a Sleeping Evangelist.

WHAT IS A SLEEPING EVANGELIST?

An Evangelist by nature is a person who seeks to convert others to the Christian faith, especially by public preaching.

A *Sleeping Evangelist* - is a person who seeks to convert others to the Christian faith, AND/OR seeks to be an *example* of the Christian faith, however they are sleeping with the very person they are trying to minister to; or has the reputation of being a 'church girl' who sleeps around with men both in and outside of the church.

Are you her? Were you her? Do you know one like her? At one point in my life I was her, and yes, to this day I still know *many* like her. Many church going Christians are actively having premarital sex. *This* is why I could not write the book without addressing this epidemic! A study completed in 2011 by The National Campaign to Prevent Teen and Unplanned Pregnancy revealed that 88% of unmarried young adults (ages 18-29) are having sex, and of those surveyed who self-identify as "evangelical," **80%** say **they have had sex**.[3]

These statistics only reveal the percentage of young adults ages 18-29, but does not address the additional number of Christians over the age of 30. Considering that the average age when people lose their virginity is

16-17 years old, it is likely that the pattern of premarital sex persists within the adult and seasoned saints as well.

THE POWER OF SEX

Sex is a gift given to husband and wife for procreation, intimacy, companionship, physical pleasure and more. Sex is not a sin, it is a gift! God honors sex and it is pleasing in His sight only when it takes place within the confines of marriage. When two people have sex outside of the context of marriage, or when they have extramarital sex, they are committing a sin against God and their own bodies. Amongst many benefits of sex within marriage, I have shared four benefits below with a scripture to support each one.

Procreation: Sex is the means by which a husband and wife can reproduce and have children. In Genesis, after God created man and woman in His own likeness, He blessed them and said, *Be fruitful and increase in number; fill the earth and subdue it.* - Genesis 1:28

Intimacy: An intimate relationship is one that implies a deep level of familiarity and personal connection. Sex leads to intimacy and brings a man and woman together as close as can be and the two become ONE. Genesis 2:24 says "*That is why a man leaves his father* *and mother and is united to his wife, and they become* ***one flesh.***"

Companionship & Unity: A Bond Established:
Scripture verses throughout Song of Solomon demonstrate how a bond of companionship is formed through a marital sexual relationship.

All night long on my bed
I looked for the one my ***heart loves****;*
I looked for him but did not find him.
2 *I will get up now and go about the city,*
through its streets and squares;
I will ***search for the one my heart loves****.*
- Song of Solomon 3:1-2

You have stolen my heart*, my sister, my bride;*
you have stolen my heart
with one glance of your eyes,
with one jewel of your necklace.
10 ***How delightful is your love****, my sister, my bride!*
How much more pleasing is your love than wine,
and the fragrance of your perfume
more than any spice! All night long on my bed
I looked for the one my heart loves;
- Song of Solomon 4:9-10

Physical Pleasure: The bible gives husbands and wives permission to enjoy themselves in the bedroom and states that "Marriage is honorable in all, and the bed undefiled" (Hebrews 13:4 KJV). The bible encourages husband and wife to have sex as it is written in 1 Corinthians 7:5 *Do not deprive each other except perhaps by mutual consent and for a time, so that you may devote yourselves to prayer. Then come together again so that Satan will not tempt you because of your lack of self-control.*

As you see, sex is very powerful! When you reflect on just the four outcomes above, you must also consider that the same is true even when you have sex with a person to whom you are not married. When you have premarital sex, you place yourself at risk for procreating and having a baby out of wedlock. You become intimately connected with the man you have sex with, essentially becoming ONE FLESH with him. A bond of companionship is established, which is strong like glue and will keep you connected and searching for more of him just like in the scriptures above. You will experience a level of sexual satisfaction and pleasure simply because of the way your body is designed to respond to touch, plus God intends for it to be pleasurable!

The affects that sex has on a husband and wife are greatly beneficial in the context of marriage! Marriage was created to last for a lifetime, so sexual intimacy, companionship, and pleasure are essential in keeping the two together. These same affects which are beneficial for the married couple are detrimental to a single (unmarried) person because sex keeps you attached to an individual who God had never intended for you to be with. Each time you have sex, you are becoming one with them, "marrying" them spiritually. Just think about it, how can you expect God to send you the man He is preparing just for you, when you are already ONE with another man and possibly many others?

THE EFFECTS OF BEING A SLEEPING EVANGELIST

The effects of being a sleeping evangelist are two-fold. First, you are establishing bonds and exchanging spirits with the very people/person you are having sex with. Secondly, you are adversely impacting the lives of the men you are sleeping with by being a stumbling block to them. Truth is, I was a stumbling block to men I was involved with too. You and I were both causing men to stumble in their walk with Christ because we were actively engaging in a sinful act with them. You must remember that every man you meet is your fellow brother in Christ first, before any other title is established. This is something I hadn't truly realized for years. Just like you, the men you are/have been sexually involved with were created by God to give Him glory through his life. Just like God died for you, He also died on the cross for him so that he may have eternal life if he believes in Jesus as his personal savior.

With this in mind, when you (and me), a Christian woman have (had) sex with a Christian man, you are helping him sin against God and his own body. As you know, sin creates distance between us and God, therefore as a result, you are aiding in creating a lack of intimacy between him and the Lord God Almighty. Let me tell you, when God spoke this to me one day, I was completely heartbroken. I didn't even realize the impact of my decisions. I engaged in sex because I wanted to be loved and I thought I was expressing love. I later learned that while engaging in premarital sex as an expression of love, I was coming in between the relationship my brother in Christ had with His first love, God. Was this *really* what I wanted? Is this *really* what *you* want to do as a Christian woman? I am positive that it's not.

Now in some cases, the Sleeping Evangelist may find herself sexually involved with an unbeliever. In the case of having a sexual relationship with an unbeliever, it still remains true that you are not representing Christ well. Many unbelievers already think Christianity is a joke and that Christians are hypocrites. Many men are attracted to "church girls" because they have gained the reputation of being "freaks in private". By having sex with him, you are only justifying his beliefs, and this is not good. His involvement with you can potentially decrease the likelihood that he will recognize that sex before marriage is sin, because he is engaging in sex with a woman who calls herself a Christian. I do not share this with you to condemn you, but I share this with you to give you another perspective on what happens when you (and I) have sex with a man who is not our husband. I've actually had a man question my "Christianity" and relationship with God because of my actions. Can you imagine that? Can you blame him either? It was in that moment that I wanted to make a rebuttal, but I was quieted by the Holy Spirit, and challenged to examine the impact I was making on his life as I was the one who carried the name of Christ.

THE EFFECTS SEX HAS ON YOUR PREPARATION

When you are engaging in premarital sex, no matter the rate of occurrence, you are prohibiting yourself from being in position and prepared for your future husband. As I shared with you above, even though you are not married, you still become united with each person you have had sex with and may be having sex with now. Prayerfully, after reading this chapter there will not be any future partners on the list. Because of the invisible bond that exists between you and your sexual partners, the natural response to this bond is emotional, physical, mental, and sexual attachment. If you have found it difficult for you to 'pull away' from one or more of your past partners or if you find yourself always running back to them, it is because you have a 'marital bond' with them that was only designed to exist between a husband and wife. There is a sexual soul tie that must be broken!

You can try to move forward in your life and maybe you have even been celibate for quite some time, however if the sexual bonds/soul ties have not been broken, then you are still carrying pieces of them with you. The profound thing about sex is that spirits are transferred through the very act. These spirits are 'tied' to you in a sense, until they are broken off supernaturally in the spirit realm. If there are certain habits you have now, that you did not have before, specific desires (contrary to the Word of God) that you never had to battle before, if there are character traits you find yourself demonstrating that are flawed, all of which were not present before engaging in premarital sex - it is likely that what you are experiencing is the result of soul ties. Remember, each time you have sex with a person you are taking on his flesh. The spirits/demons on him have been/are being transferred to you and will not be released until the invisible bond has been broken. Barbara Wilson, author of *The Invisible Bond* puts it this way, "Long after the lover is gone, the bond we've created stays with us, impacting our lives and future relationship in a negative way....The greater the number of sexual partners, the greater the harmful residue, and the greater the long-term impact." [4]

You see, as much as you may beg to differ, sex is not just an event of pleasure that has no effect on your life.

Even though you can ask God for forgiveness, it does not mean that you will be exempt from the consequences of your sin.

I encourage you, for the sake of your relationship with God and your future, to recommit yourself to purity. Even if you have sex once every 3 months, or one time a year, that one experience will have a greater impact on you than what meets the eye. Moreover, sex blinds you and clouds your vision. After having sex, even one time with a guy, it is likely that you begin to think he's "The One". You may have already experienced this. Of course this can easily happen because you have indeed become "one" with him. When you have sex, this also causes you to ignore and overlook red flags. Because of the level of companionship and intimacy you have shared and the bond created, you cannot even see the facts about him because your flesh is one with him.

There is so much more to discuss about sex, but that will be for another time. Right now, I want to share with you how the invisible bonds of sex (soul ties) can be BROKEN! This is so very important as you desire to be married. You want to enter into a covenant with your husband having broken the bond with previous partners. Not doing so before marriage, will cause you to literally drag the residue from others into your marriage, and you do not want this. Let me be the first to tell you that bonds can be broken, you can be new, and YOU CAN change! I am a testament of God's TRANSFORMATIONAL power!

As you may have gathered from reading this book, I have had my fair share of unrighteousness and living to please my flesh. Not many people were aware of my secret struggles, because again, I was wearing a mask. However, there came a point in my life when I just could not take it anymore! I was tired of being the typical "church girl". I was sick of my sin. I wanted to be made over. I wanted to live a pure lifestyle. I desired a closer relationship with God *more* than I wanted to fulfill my fleshly desires. I had a deep desperation for more of God and I wanted to please Him in EVERY area of my life.

Do you desire the same? Are you ready to break the cycle of the sleeping evangelist? Do you want to be free of the bonds of sexual immorality? Are you ready to break the soul ties that exist between you and men you have had sex with? I pray that your answer is "YES!"

THE GOOD NEWS!

YOU CAN BE RENEWED!

YOU CAN BE SET FREE!

THERE IS HOPE!

YOU CAN BE REDEEMED!

YOU CAN BE TRANSFORMED!

God did it for me, and I know He will do it for you! You do not have to continue to struggle as the secret sleeping evangelist!

You CAN BE F-R-E-E!

The amazing news about God is that He is a loving, gracious, and forgiving God! God desires that you live a righteous lifestyle and He will RENEW you completely if you allow! The Renewed & Ready4TheRing Movement was actually birthed and inspired by God's power to RENEW! One of my favorite scriptures, which is also and foundational scripture for the Renewed & Ready4TheRing Movement is Psalm 51:10 *Create in me a clean heart, O God; and* ***renew*** *a right spirit within me.*

This scripture was spoken to God by David. David was considered a man after God's own heart. David was a disciple of Christ, God used him in mighty ways, and David sinned against God and his own body when he slept with Bathsheba. David committed adultery and murder. What I love about David's story is that he recognized his shortcomings and sin. He knew he needed to change and could only do so with God's help! He was repentant and sorry for living in such a way that did not glorify God. David cried out and prayed to the Lord! He believed and asked God to extend His grace, mercy, and forgiveness, and God did just that! Just like David, I did the very same thing!

I cried out to the Lord one evening with a repentant heart, a contrite spirit, and with a pure desire to please Him and to be made whole. I asked Him to forgive me of my sexual sin and to create in me a clean heart and RENEW a right spirit within me! As I continued to pray to Him, I began to feel the burden of guilt and shame lift as His forgiveness, love, mercy, and grace showered down on me. I knew I could not change on my own. I knew I needed His Spirit to guide me, help me, heal me, restore me, and empower me. God is able to make *you* NEW again! You do not have to continue to live the way that you are, or the way you once did. God can RENEW you too! He can break the soul ties and invisible bonds that exist in your life! It is time for you to be Renewed & Ready4TheRing!

HOW TO BREAK THE BONDS OF SEX

If you are actively having sex, or have had sex before but are celibate now, I want to share with you 5 steps I personally followed to break free of the bonds of sex and soul ties I had in my life. As you desire to break free from your bonds, I recommend you do the same!

You may think that breaking soul ties means that you must be at the altar with multiple Holy Ghost filled, fire-baptized, tongue-speaking, prophetic giving, laying-on-of-hands ministers, elders, and pastors encircled about you. While there is nothing wrong with this method, I do not want you to think that this scene and experience is the only way to be delivered and have soul ties broken from your life. There are many people who are subject to the altar workers who leave the church the same way they went in. Not because the ministers did anything wrong, but because the individual's heart was not right. They were not sincere, they wanted a quick fix, and they may not have even had the faith needed for God to move on their behalf. I want you to know that God can break the sexual bonds and soul ties right there where you are, right now! He can do it with just you and Him. As long as you put your trust and total faith in Him and His process, He will do just what you ask!

Here are **5 steps to break free of the bonds of sex and soul ties**

Step One: Submit

Submit means to yield or surrender (oneself) to the will or authority of another. In order to position yourself for chains and soul ties to be broken, you must surrender to God. You must surrender your will and recognize God's will for you. When you do this, you are making yourself available unto Him so that He may transform you from the inside-out.

Step Two: Confess

Because you have decided to no longer live life on your own terms, but according to God's will- you now recognize that premarital sex is a sin against God and your own body.

By an act of opening your mouth and speaking to God, admitting that your lifestyle is not pleasing to Him, and that you have sinned, you are confessing to God. Confession causes you to be vulnerable and open to God. You also become truthful about what you've done and honest with yourself about your decisions. Confession leads to forgiveness. When you confess your sins, God is faithful and just to forgive you (1 John 1:9).

Step Three: Repent

Repentance is a change of heart and mind that brings us closer to God. It includes turning away from **sin** and turning to God for forgiveness. Repent refers to a change. As it relates to breaking the bond of sex, you turn from pleasing your flesh to being committed to pleasing God. Remember, in the first step, you surrendered your will. Now in this step, you are dedicating yourself to following after God. Once your mind is renewed, you think differently, and you do differently. You change.

Step Four: Pray

Prayer is simply a conversation with God. Talk to God. Specifically pray for these four things: forgiveness, freedom, cleansing, purification, and restoration. Write out a sexual history list with names of people you have been sexually involved in any way with and write anything else that God shows you. Ask God to forgive your sin and to free you of all sexual bonds that have been created both known and unknown to you. Ask God to cleanse you and remove all habits, thought patterns and anything that has attached itself to you through sexual experiences you've had. Pray for God to make you over in His image and create in you a clean heart and right spirit.

Step Five: Obey

The bible says that obedience is better than sacrifice (1 Samuel 15:22). You can sacrifice your time and do all of the above steps, however if you do not obey God's commands and His will, then you will continue to find yourself in the cycle of the Sleeping Evangelist. Once you ask, believe, and declare that soul ties are broken, you must now be committed to living a pure lifestyle as His words commands. Obeying God simply means aligning yourself with His Word, allowing Him to lead you, and following Him because you know His plan for you is the best plan! God's Word lets us know that the way we show God we love Him is through our obedience. John 14:15 says *If ye love me, keep my commandments.*

BECOME A BETTER WOMAN

Preparing yourself for marriage has to do with you becoming a better woman so that you can be a better wife. Having a sexual bond with one or more persons who is not your husband prohibits you from being a better woman and from being in position for your husband to find you. Additionally, having premarital sex of any kind is contrary to the Word of God and His will for you. Decide today to no longer be the typical 'church girl'. It is actually disheartening that women in the church have such a hypocritical reputation. YOU can start to show the world that you are a woman of integrity and honor! Start by asking God to set you free and to break the bonds of the sexual experiences you've had up until today!

Remember: A woman, who is positioned to be found, is not positioned in a bed with a man who is not her husband. She is positioned with purity, purpose, and prayer!

Ready4TheRing Plan of Action?
Break The Bonds and Habits of Sex!

- ❖ Search the scriptures to gain a better understanding about what the bible says about sex. Take note on what is honorable to God and what displeases Him.

- ❖ Begin the process of breaking free of sexual bonds and soul ties.

- ❖ Ask God to help you see your sin with His eyes.

- ❖ List the names of persons you were involved with sexually. Prepare to call these names out one by one as you pray for forgiveness and freedom of soul ties.

- ❖ Pray that your heart will be humbled so that you enter the process and pray with sincerity and not out of habit or tradition.

- ❖ Review the 5 steps above and pray to God with each step as a focus in your prayer. You can pray this prayer or a similar one:

Dear Lord, I thank you because you are so good! I thank you because you are a forgiving, merciful, and gracious God. I come to you first submitting myself to you. I need you Lord.

I have done things on my own and outside of your will especially as it relates to men, and I confess that I have sinned against you with my body. I have even sinned against my own body by having sex. Lord I repent, and I desire to change my ways so that I follow you and no longer give into my flesh and worldly desires. I am sorry for having sex outside of marriage. Please forgive me Lord.

Through sex, many desires, habits, spirits, and thoughts that are not of you have attached themselves to me. In the name of Jesus, I pray for freedom from every desire, mindset, habit, spirit, and soul tie! By your power I ask you to break every bond, attachment, soul tie, and chain created as I engaged in sexual contact and/or intercourse with ________________.

Lord, Just as you've forgiven me, I choose today to forgive ______________ for the abuse, misuse, and/or violation against me. I also pray that you would empower me to forgive myself for all that I have done. Please renew me, make me over, cleanse me, and purify me, so that I can be made brand new. Heal me of my brokenness both known and unknown, and wash me of all guilt, shame, regret, and more. I believe your Word which says that I can ask anything in your name according to your word, and it shall be done. So today, I declare that I am free of sexual bonds and all soul ties are broken! I am renewed! I am restored! I am redeemed! And I am forgiven!

In Jesus' name I pray, Amen.

- ❖ Commit to reading the book *The Invisible Bond* by Barbara Wilson. This book will help you understand more about sexual bonds and being free!

- ❖ Seek and ask God to reveal to you a trusted accountability partner who is a sister-in-Christ that will continue to pray with you and for you. You can read God's Word together, fast, and support one another as you both strive to live a pure lifestyle.

- ❖ Continue to remember this day! Remember that you are free! Commit to God's will for your life and rely on his strength as you determine to live a pure lifestyle.

NOTES:

Chapter 9: The Power of Boundaries

❖ *Jewel of Wisdom:*

Boundaries are designed to protect and prevent. Determine your emotional and physical boundaries before your next relationship so you can protect your purity, prevent heartbreak, and position yourself to be a bride.
#Ready4TheRing

Now that we have discussed sex, this is a perfect time to talk more about boundaries! We know that sex is reserved for married couples, and prayerfully after reading the previous chapter, you have made a vow to recommit yourself to purity. Does this mean that you can do whatever you want and engage in every act that leads to sex, but not have sex? Some would say sure, but I believe God desires that you still honor Him with your body beyond not having premarital sex. In order to do so, you must have boundaries established.

Boundaries do not limit you or keep you bound. They actually serve to protect you!

If you reflect on the relationships that did not work out as planned, and recall the heartbreak and pain you experienced due to the failed relationship, you may begin to see that there were some precautionary measures you could have taken to protect your heart more than you did. The truth is, we often limit the principle of boundaries. We typically focus on the importance of establishing physical boundaries only; however, it is important that you determine **emotional**, **time**, **language**, **mental**, and **material** boundaries also! YES! There are a variety of boundaries that I'm encouraging you to set so that you protect and prevent yourself from progressing in a relationship with someone who does not have your best interest in mind and who will prohibit you from being in position to be found by your husband. Boundaries must be set in each stage of a relationship: acquaintances, friendship, dating, courtship, engagement, and even in marriage, but that's for another time.

WHY BOUNDARIES ARE IMPORTANT

With marriage as your desire, you must understand that the establishment of boundaries leads you to the path of becoming a bride, and without boundaries you avert your availability to be found by your husband. Let me explain. Without appropriate boundaries while you are single, you become susceptible to counterfeit relationships and being distracted by both your feelings and heart. Furthermore, when appropriate boundaries are not predefined and you have fallen subject to the emotional connection you have with a man who is not your husband, then you are unable to recognize The One God has for you because you are preoccupied!

I mentioned earlier that boundaries are necessary in all levels of relationship. When you do not have appropriate boundaries per level of relationship, it is likely you will end up heartbroken in the end because the level of relationship was not clearly defined outside of just the title.

TYPES OF BOUNDARIES

EMOTIONAL BOUNDARIES: Emotions are simply *strong feelings*. Examples of emotions are love, joy, hate, fear, sadness, excitement, and more. When relating to a man, your emotions toward him (strong feelings) develop only as you allow them to. Typically if you like a man, the emotions you feel are that of admiration, love, happiness, joy, excitement, and more!

Although mainstream media tries to deceive you into thinking otherwise, I need you to know that you indeed have power to control your feelings.

You cannot control them yourself, because your emotions are tainted by your sinful nature. But you need the power of God and the Holy Spirit within you to control your emotions so that you operate according to the Spirit and not your flesh (Romans 8:9-11). Without the appropriate measures or limitations, you will mislead yourself into believing that you must come subject to your feelings, even though feelings are fickle (unpredictable, inconsistent, changeable). Having emotional boundaries means that you will monitor your emotions, not allowing yourself to be overtaken by the feelings you experience when dealing with a man. You will not allow your feelings to control you, causing you to be irrational in your thinking and decision making. Your emotions can easily run rampant when your heart is not saturated in scripture.

When establishing emotional boundaries for yourself, you must reflect on the level of your relationship with a man and determine if the feelings you have are in rightful alignment with your relationship status. When the two do not align, heartbreak and disappointment are the result.

TIME BOUNDARIES: I've heard it said like this, time is one thing you cannot get back. As a single woman, you must reevaluate how you spend your time, and on whom you spend your time. Naturally, the more time you spend with a person, the more likely it is that you will develop feelings for them. There is no need to spend hours upon hours with a person of the opposite sex when the two of you are 'just friends'. Some women spend much more time with a male friend than they do with their female friends! This is not good! When you allow a man to spend a lot of time with you before a true commitment, you are allowing him access into your life which he should not have.

Your time is precious girl! There are more things for you to do with your time than sit around and cuddle, watch TV, and hang out with a man who is not your husband quite yet! Get busy serving God and His people! Use your time to build your ministry and your brand. Carve out time to write your book, visit the sick & shut in, and operate in your purpose! There is more to do with your time than allow a man to fill it all up! This is why many women end up with much regret after they realize they have wasted time giving their time to a man who was not fully committed and did not marry them in the end! I encourage you to be WISE with your time. You cannot get it back. A man who desires to be your husband will not want to steal all of your time. Yes, he will want to spend time with you, rightfully so, but he will not desire to be a distraction from what it is that God is calling you to! That's a RED FLAG if he is trying to steal your time away from your purpose, family, friends, church, and from you reaching your goals. As you matriculate through the levels of relationship, the time you spend together with your mate will increase, but more importantly the quality of time should amplify! Quality vs. Quantity is important!

LANGUAGE BOUNDARIES: Yes, ma'am! Language boundaries must exist! The way in which the two of you speak to one another must be monitored: tone of voice, word choice, and the type of conversation you share. We all know that the tone of a man's voice can make a woman go wild! (Either in a positive way or negative way) Likewise, the tone of your voice when speaking to a man will tell him a lot. It's important to manage your tone of voice so that it is appropriate for the level of relationship you are in. For example, I have witnessed women speak to a man with a small, sweet, flirtatious whispering voice but yet she claims him as her "'brother" or friend. *Sorry sis, you're talking to him like he's your spouse during a romantic candlelight dinner.* Talk about *leading a man on!* Likewise, a man may talk to his fiancé with a harsh tone like he's out on the football field coaching and she may feel disrespected or question his sensitivity. It is important that the tone of voice being used is appropriate for the relationship.

Word choice is another principle under language boundaries. Using words like "boo", "babe", "love", "honey", "sweetheart" and other names of admiration need to be reserved for when you are in an exclusive relationship. You and your man should not refer to each other as such when you are only dating. If he addresses you as such, he is probably calling the other ladies he is dating the same thing! Use of these terms of endearment too early will cause you to misinterpret the level of relationship because your title is one thing, but your language suggests another. This is the same for use of those three words "I love you". People use these words very loosely nowadays, but these words get people, especially us women tripped up! If a man is telling you this and he has not made an exclusive commitment to you - RED FLAG! He probably doesn't mean it sincerely. If he did truly love you, he would demonstrate his love by being fully committed to you and relinquish his connections with other women!

Lastly, when it comes to language boundaries: be mindful of the types of conversations you allow yourself to have with a man! This is vitally important. Sometimes we talk too much! We tell too much! Then we wonder why it is so easy for this man to meet your "needs" without him giving you a ring! You do not need to tell a man what turns you on, what sexual positions you like, what you look for in a man, how to make you feel good, etc. That type of conversation is a violation of each level of relationship outside of marriage. Additionally, you need to reserve "marriage & wedding talk" for after he has proposed to you! You may think he's your husband, you may want to marry him, he may even entertain the conversation, but until he gets on one knee to propose, tame your tongue! Do not let yourself engage in conversations such as this and discuss family plans, etc. This will cause you to put the "horse before the cart". You are "counting your chickens before they hatch". Do you see why you need to have language boundaries?

MENTAL BOUNDARIES: Mental boundaries are limitations you put on yourself and they really have nothing to do with the man. Many times, women do not monitor their thoughts, which include daydreams and fantasies. If you sit around and think, fantasize, and daydream about all the possibilities and potential your relationship with a man can bring, you are doing yourself a disservice. Unless that man is fully committed to making you his wife through his demonstration of his love and his action steps toward proposing to you - you will be sorry you did this. It is so easy for us to allow our thoughts to go wild, because we always hope for a *happily-ever-after* ending, but we do not live in a fairytale world. Relationships do not always end this way. So I encourage you, to check yourself! Before you continue to allow a man to occupy your thoughts, remember what the bible says, *Finally, brothers and sisters, whatever is true, whatever is noble, whatever is right, whatever is pure, whatever is lovely, whatever is admirable—if anything is excellent or praiseworthy--think about such things* (Philippians 4:8). The bible also says to meditate on the Word day and night (Joshua 1:8). It is the Word of God and His truths that you ought to consistently fill your thoughts with, not a man and your wedding day. Refocus your mind! This will help you avoid living in false hope (you *remember that chapter, right?)*

MATERIAL BOUNDARIES: Gifts are great, but we know gifts symbolize one's thoughtfulness and kindness toward another. If a man is giving you gifts, and you are only acquaintances - you may be tempted to take them. Honey, don't do it! He is not giving you gifts without reason. It is likely he is trying to win you over and he wants to know you better as a girlfriend at least. If the feelings are mutual, sure accept the gift - your relationship may move to the next level, but if you do not feel the same way, politely refuse it. If not, you will be leading him on and/or he may become infatuated with you and this is not cool at all.

Material boundaries also include limiting the amount of possessions you share with a man. If you all are sharing a home/apartment, a car, a bank account, a bill, and more without having said your vows, you are crossing the boundaries! The above should not even take place during the season of being engaged to be married, so you know it definitely should not happen with less commitment than that. Remember, when the level of relationship is not in alignment with the level of interaction & interpersonal connections, someone is bound to get hurt. More than likely it will be you because women are more emotional than men. So play it safe, do not cross material boundaries.

PHYSICAL BOUNDARIES: I believe you know that physical boundaries must be established in order to uphold being recommitted to celibacy. With this, I want to briefly discuss having physical boundaries well before sex even takes place. Think about it. It is rare that two people look at each other and then the next second they are having sex. No, there is typically a natural progression of other physical contact which happens first. Let's talk about that along with the levels of relationship.

Holding hands to some may be an act that is harmless or is a simple action that means nothing at all. In actuality a hormone called oxytocin is released when two people hold hands. It is a hormone that cements long term relationship and raises the amount of affection in a couple. So think about this the next time you hold hands with a male "friend" or your date. If you begin to wonder why your attraction increases, think about the oxytocin!

In addition to holding hands, it is important to be mindful that during hugs, snuggles, and cuddles, (and even sex) this same hormone is released. Because the hormone raises the amount of affection in a couple, do you think it's wise not to have physical boundaries when it comes to men? I don't think so. Physical connection of any kind will always have a greater impact on a woman because of the hormone we release and also because typically our emotions get involved with physical activities of any kind. Because men are more sexual creatures, they can engage in physical activities without emotional connection. This is why a man and woman can have sex, the relationship end, but the woman is still emotionally attached (not to mention soul ties).

Physical interactions must be reserved for exclusive relationships only. At this time, I will not get into what level of physical actions is permitted, but I will say that the establishment of physical boundaries is imperative! I will also reiterate that any and all types of sexual intercourse are strictly prohibited and reserved for marriage only.

WHY BOUNDARIES ARE IMPORTANT

Boundaries protect you! Boundaries keep you emotionally safe! Boundaries lead you down the path of becoming a bride. Like standards, boundaries are actually respected by a Man of God who wants to marry an honorable woman of God. A man that cannot respect your boundaries does not deserve to have you as their bride.

Boundaries create the parameters of each level of relationship you can experience. You do not want blurred-boundaries. When boundaries are blurred, a woman easily becomes heartbroken.

Here are a few more reasons why you want to have boundaries established:

- When boundaries are established you can better recognize the red flags in relationships.

Once certain boundaries are crossed when dealing with men, it can become more difficult to see clearly. You can become blinded because confines have been crossed. This can cause a woman to overlook the warning signs and flaws in a man, when she should not.

- Lack of boundaries causes you to be too available to the man, making it easy for him to take advantage of you.

Once a man knows he can get more from you than what he should have, he will not commit fully to you! Why does he need to be your fiancé, when he gets full access to you as a friend? He will use you up until there is no more of you to give.

- Lack of boundaries will lead you farther away from being prepared for the one God has for you.

The danger of not having boundaries, or boundaries being crossed, is that your level of admiration and desire for more of them increases. This stands true for the types of boundaries mentioned above. Being connected to a man who is not your husband, will cause you not to be in position for God's best gift for you! When you are connected with a man in any way who is not your husband, God is unable to prepare you for marriage because you are emotionally, mentally, and spiritually unavailable.

When you do not have appropriate boundaries, you become so wrapped up in a man that you ignore God himself. He can't even get to you because your attention is solely focused on your "boo".

It is totally possible to be involved in a relationship with a man and adhere to and uphold suitable boundaries for your relationship. When you do this, your emotions, time, language, mind, possessions, and physical body is still under God's rule. Your emotions, time, language, mind, possessions, and physical body have not been overtaken by your fleshly desires, and sinful nature.

Overall, the establishment of boundaries when in relationship with men on any level helps you:

- ✓ Maintain a man's respect
- ✓ Protect your heart
- ✓ Prohibit yourself from falling 'in too deep'
- ✓ Keeps your mind focused on God and His will for you

- ✓ Give a man something to look forward to in marriage

If every man you date, are attracted to, or are in a relationship with has had access to your emotions, time, language (flirtatious tone of voice, terms of endearment, & candid conversations), your mind, materials, and physical body - what would be left for exclusive sharing between you and your husband? My sister, boundaries of each kind are indeed essential to your own personal & spiritual growth, but also in your desire to be a bride. Once you become a bride, you can give your ALL. Until then, you must limit what you give and allow men to have access to, for your own protection, preparation, and positioning.

Ready4TheRing Plan Of Action:
Be Committed to Boundaries

- ❖ Review the types of boundaries we discussed. Identify the top 3 categories you tend to have the most difficulty upholding.

- ❖ Pray, repent, and ask God to forgive you for allowing men more access to you than you should have. Be specific in your prayer by calling out the category in which you have not upheld appropriate boundaries.

- In your journal, make a table with all the categories. After considerable thought and reflection, list your newly-defined boundaries under each category. Be specific.

- Pray and ask God to empower you to uphold appropriate boundaries when dealing with men. Be specific in asking Him to help you in the areas where you have previously had difficulty. Commit to the boundaries you have established.

NOTES:

Part 3:

Prepare And Position Yourself

Chapter 10: Discerning Distractions

❖ *Jewel of Wisdom:*

Not every man is sent by God. Most are sent by Satan as a distraction. He gives 'gifts' too, however, they are counterfeit. You must be aware that the enemy is determined to divert your focus and keep you from being in God's perfect will. Because of this, it is imperative that you seek God, pray, and use discernment so you do not entertain a distraction. #Ready4TheRing

I see it all the time. I have had the opportunity to speak with many women and it happens quite often that they are connected with a man who has done nothing for them but keep them distracted. Of course, they do not usually recognize this until they have engaged in an honest self-evaluation and reflection with me as their coach. Let me tell you, I have been guilty of this too. I have learned that desiring to be married is one thing, but actually waiting for God to send you your husband is another. In a world that is flooded with the ability to see a glimpse into other's lives, it is so easy to desire what other women have.

At the click of a mouse, or scroll on our phone, we see our friends making social media posts about what appears to be moments of happiness captured from an evening of romance and enjoyment. We watch television shows and movies that display intimate connections, friendships, and relationships that project ideas of love and affection. We listen to music which permeates our minds with endless visions and dreams of being wrapped in a man's arms while he caresses our bodies with a gentle, sensual touch. What we see with our eyes begins to increase our desire for that same love experience. Within seconds, we find ourselves longing for a connection with a man who will fulfill every fantasy of love and romance in our mind. We become what some call *hopeless romantics,* and each day we aspire to attain love; with great anticipation for love and marriage, we just can't wait for our turn. I hear it all the time and these words use to slide off my tongue and reside in my mind as well:

"Oooo I can't wait until I get married!"

"I can't wait until I have a boyfriend."

"I can't wait until I have a husband."

"Girl, I can't wait until I can have sex (without feeling guilty or having to run to the altar afterwards)!...My husband will not be disappointed."

While you say these statements out of your excitement as you are waiting for your turn to come, you are also underestimating the power of the words that came out of your mouth. When you say "I can't wait until I have a boyfriend" and other statements alike, you must realize that you literally just said "<u>I can't wait</u>", and so though you are not conscious of it at the time - you just spoke a destructive declaration into the atmosphere and over your life. Now, because you have said <u>*I can't wait*</u>, *you* actually *don't* wait! If you are wondering why you are experiencing such difficulty waiting, think about your words!

HAVE YOUR WORDS WELCOMED YOUR DISTRACTIONS? HAVE YOU *TRULY* BEEN WAITING TO BE FOUND?

Think about it. You may have said with excitement, ***"Oooo I can't wait until I get married!"***

<u>Now ask yourself these questions:</u>

- Have I been acting like I am married while I am dating or in a relationship? **Just in case you* *don't know what this looks like, here are a few questions to determine your answer**

- Have I waited until marriage to be in a relationship where I give my *ALL*?

- Have I ever given all my love, time, and energy to a man who has not given me his last name?

- Have I exhausted myself trying to keep a relationship intact so that we would not break up and stay together forever?

If you have answered YES to any of these questions, this is a sign that you have not been successfully waiting until marriage to engage in the emotional, spiritual, and physical connection that should only exist between a husband and wife. From this moment forward, I encourage you not to say "I can't wait until marriage". Instead say "I want to be ready for marriage" or "I am looking forward to marriage".

Maybe you have said, ***"I can't wait until I have a boyfriend."***

Ask yourself these questions:

- Have I spent time talking to guys that did not actually fulfill the standards I once had?

- Do I find myself lowering my expectations in order to be with a guy?

- Do I spend time with male "friends" secretly hoping that they will make it official with me one day?

If you have said yes to either one of these questions, this a good indicator that you were willing to release your core principles in a mate in order to fulfill a personal desire of having a boyfriend, or someone to spend time with, cuddle with, and go on dates with. I need you to know that YES *you can* indeed <u>wait</u> to have a boyfriend. You *can wait* until God connects you with a man of good character. You *can wait* for someone to pursue you without compromising. Stop saying "you can't wait" because then you won't wait.

Even if you have not said it, you may have thought something like this:

"I can't wait until I have a husband." or
"Girl, I can't wait until I can have sex without guilt... My husband will not be disappointed."

<u>Now ask yourself these questions:</u>

- Am I a virgin?

- Have I had sex of any kind before?

- Have I lived with a guy before, or have I stayed overnight with one?

If you answered each question honestly, you will begin to see how the power of your desires and your words have dictated and influenced your decisions and actions. Just like me at one point, you have probably never thought that by expressing your dreams you shape your life to an extent. You see, we know that our words have power, but we tend to only apply this concept to statements we make that are favorable such as "I will have a new job next year" or "I will be an entrepreneur and make millions". This chapter is not about the power of your words, but this concept is very important as I delve deeper into distractions.

THE TRUTH ABOUT DISTRACTIONS

I mention all of this to you to demonstrate how our desires and the way in which we declare them have a strong ability to create or result in distractions. Having a desire to be married is perfectly fine; however, know that distractions come into your life as Satan's way to deter you from being in position for your husband to find you and for you to recognize him.

I want to share with you a few definitions of distractions. **Distraction** is defined as:

(1) A thing that prevents someone from giving full attention to something else
(2) A diversion
(3) Extreme agitation of the mind or emotions
(4) Something that makes it difficult to think or pay attention (Merriam-Webster Online)

For purposes of this book, a **<u>distraction</u>** prevents you from giving your full attention to someone else (God, and His will for your life AND your true desire to be a wife), it agitates your mind and emotions, and it is a diversion, which makes it difficult for you to think or pay attention.

Does this sound like some of the men you have been involved with either in the past, recently, or even right now? As women, many times we avoid admitting that someone who we like, or the connection we have with a man, was <u>sent</u> as a distraction. As you desire to be married, you cannot forget that marriage was created and ordained by God. Satan is the enemy of our soul, he hates God, and he does not want you to attain God's blessings nor be in His will. In an effort to keep you from being in position to be married (which is God's holy ordnance) Satan will send distractions (a man) your way. Remember, because you spoke in the atmosphere that you just *"can't wait"* for a husband, boyfriend, sex, etc. you have given Satan direct access to your weakness. Yes, he knows the very areas in which to attack you, causing you to step outside of God's will for you so that you can experience your desire of love, affection, admiration without having said your vows.

This chapter is about distractions. As we talk about distractions, we must address the fact that distractions are not of God, nor from God. The bible says that Satan comes to steal, kill, and destroy (John 10:10). There are no limitations or specifications to what he will demolish. While you have the desire to marry God's best for you, Satan is prowling around like a lion looking for someone to devour (1 Peter 5:8). As it relates to marriage, you are in his radar as he seeks to *steal* your focus, *kill* your ability to wait on God for your husband, and *destroy* your sexual purity and your capacity to trust God's timing. He is also determined to divert your desire to wait, causing you to give into your flesh. He does all of this and more, while fulfilling the description of a **distraction** because he sends men to "*agitate (stir up) your mind and emotions*", and while you are in relationships, he makes it difficult for you to think (logically) or pay attention (to the signs).

Satan is very skilled at what he does, and what he does will continue to be successful in the lives of women everywhere until we recognize what is truly going on. Let me tell you, nothing happens coincidentally with God, neither do distractions enter your life in that manner. Everything that happens and the men who come to you happen on purpose. As a Christian woman, it is up to you to be mindful and mature enough to use discernment in order to recognize the difference between a man sent by God as a blessing or a man sent by Satan as a distraction.

When I started this chapter, I mentioned how television and media play a large role in shaping our desires. Please remember that Satan is the ruler of the kingdom of the air (Ephesians 2:2), which means that he is in control of this earthly world and has influence over the media and television. So if Satan can negatively pollute airways, and he also hates God's ordinance of marriage, it's no wonder why he will use the media to distract us and impart in us distorted images of love and both premarital & extramarital relationships that appear to be fulfilling and rewarding!

Know this: what you feed into your life, will lead. Your surroundings and environment affect your desires, and your desires influence your decisions. This is why it is critically important to intentionally guard your heart and be mindful of what you allow into your eye and ear gates. This means to monitor what you watch and listen to because those very things have the power to overtake you. The media outlets, whether social or traditional, have major influence on the way(s) women think about themselves and relationships. As I mentioned previously, as a result, *many women are more in love with the* **idea** *of being IN love than actually experiencing TRUE love.* It is ***this*** strong aspiration and longing that very easily keeps women:

(a.) Involved in a relationship God never intended you to be in

(b.) Connected with a man that is depleting you and adds nothing but emotional baggage to your life

(c.) Engaged in a relationship that is causing distance between herself and God.

As you position yourself to be found by your husband, and prepare yourself right now, you must always keep in mind that while God wants to bless you with his best, Satan will put your ability to wait on God to the test. Remember that he is prowling around *seeking* who he may devour. Be mindful that every man that comes your way is not from God, he may be sent as a distraction. Now that Satan's plan has been exposed, you can be on guard. No more distractions for you, because you will use discernment each time a man approaches you, enters your life, or even tries to re-enter your life.

Ready4TheRing Plan Of Action:
Be On Guard: Discern Distractions

- Reflect on your current and/or previous relationships. Ask God to reveal to you the relationships and men which were sent as a distraction. A clear way to discern whether a man/relationship is a distraction is if the relationship caused you to compromise your standards, boundaries, and your walk with God. Did the relationship draw you closer to God or create distance between you and God. If the relationship caused you to function outside of God's Word and His will; if sinful thoughts and actions made up your relationship these are signs that the man/relationship was a distraction.

- Pray to God, repent, and ask God for forgiveness for allowing a man and/or your relationship to take first place in your life over Him. Ask God to help empower you to prioritize your relationship with Him.

- Surrender your will to God by letting Him know that you want to walk in His plan for your life. Ask Him to give you the spirit of discernment so that you will not be easily moved by every man that desires your attention and relationship.

Pray for His wisdom, knowledge and understanding so that you will be able to recognize Satan's tricks so you can stand against his plot for your life. Be determined to only associate yourself with men who are in alignment with God's Word and are walking in obedience to Him. This will help you avoid distractions.

NOTES:

Chapter 11: **Preparation & Positioning Prohibitors**

❖ *Jewel of Wisdom:*

Your preparation for marriage is just as much about what you prohibit in your life as it is about how you position yourself in life to be found. Decide to remove all which stands in the way of your emotional, mental, spiritual, and physical availability unto your future husband so that at God's appointed time, you will have the capacity to become ONE with him. #Ready4TheRing

As you should have been able to gather from chapters 1-10, it is what you do in this season of your singleness that will either **prepare** you emotionally, mentally, spiritually, and physically for marriage, OR **prohibit** you from being in proper position and ready to unite with God's husband for you.

It is important that you implement all which has been mentioned throughout the book and that you make a commitment to allow God to continue the renewal and transformation process He has begun in you since you have opened this book *and* your heart. This book is not a guarantee that 'once you do these things God is going to bless you!'. This book, however, was written as a guide and tool to help YOU become a better woman; one that a Christian Man/Kingdom Man/Disciple of Christ would see as a "good thing". Better women make better wives!

Below, I have identified what I refer to as the Top 10 Preparation & Positioning Prohibitors. It is these 10 habits, mindsets, and behaviors that can ultimately hinder and deter you from being prepared to become ONE with your future husband, or from being able to have yourself in proper position to receive or recognize him. As you read each one, I encourage you to be honest with yourself about where you are. If you find that these habits, mindsets, and behaviors describe you, that's great! It is not great that this is where you are, but it is great that you have identified that a prohibitor exists in your life. Once identifying the prohibitor, then you can avail yourself to God and depend on Him to transform you in this area. Let's get started, so *you can* position yourself to be #Ready4TheRing! I will give a brief description of each below. You will find that some of the prohibitors "ring a bell"!

The purpose of this chapter is to help you avoid common pitfalls and mistakes many women make.

Top 10 "Preparation & Positioning Prohibitors"

Prohibitor #1: Staying connected with your ex

This is a controversial statement, however it is impossible for you to be connected in any way to your ex, and still expect that you will be ready to connect with your husband. I don't need to go into this too deeply as we covered "Kissing the Past Goodbye" in chapter 6. Be sure to reread that chapter if this is you! Let me specify that your ex is your ex for a reason! If you all have been in relationship together and it did not work out – NO – he does not need to become one of your "friends". Your future husband will not appreciate this (even if he does not mention anything to you about it; know that this is not a sign of your honor toward him, and it is actually disrespect unto him. He should not even have to address you about your ex; when you marry, you forsake all others). I know you're not married at the moment, but while staying connected with your ex whether through conversation, un-official dates, sex, texting, and more - you are not allowing yourself to be free of the emotional connection that exists between you two. You may think you have no feelings for him or there is no bond...but if that is true - why won't you just let him go! *Something to think about!*

Simply put - you cannot prepare yourself for the next, while being connected with your ex!

Prohibitor #2: Constantly spending time with a man who is not looking for a marital commitment

When a man says that he is not ready for a commitment, it does not matter if his actions suggest otherwise, you must believe him! A man will not lie about something like this! I know these are words you really do not want to hear, but you would be wasting your time and holding on to "false hope" if you believe him. The same applies if he tells you something like "I think you're great. I love you, but I'm not sure you're the one." Listen, a man goes after what he wants! Men are designed to be 'hunters' and 'pursuers'. If he is not sure you are The One, then you can *be sure* that you are not the one. *I know, another OUCH moment, but think of it as tough love!* As my husband always says, *"Somebody's got to tell the truth around here!"* I am only trying to help you.

God is not going to send you an indecisive man. Yes, he may need to pray about whether or not you're the one - but know that once he does, God WILL speak. If that man does not come back and say with certainty that you are 'The One', but he continues to keep you around - BEWARE! WATCH OUT! I must tell you, it is likely he's determined that he does not want to marry you, but he does want to enjoy your company and benefits without a marital commitment to you. If this is happening to you, then YOU take the liberty to END the relationship. This man is double-minded and remember the bible says a *double-minded man is unstable in all his ways* (James 1:8). Is this *really* the kind of man you want to marry? *I didn't think so!* Whether this situation applies to you now, or you need to store it in your memory bank, remember - do not allow yourself to continue to be in a relationship with a man who does not want to pursue a marital commitment with you. By doing so, you are not only wasting your time, but you are prohibiting yourself from being available to a man who actually would want to marry you. You cannot be found by your husband, while in the arms of another man.

Prohibitor #3: Not attending church regularly; no commitment to a local body of believers

Because God created the Holy ordinance of marriage, if you want to be emotionally, mentally, spiritually, and physically ready to enter this covenant, then you must be in commune with Him both individually and corporately. Attending church and having a church home is vitally important to your spiritual maturity and growth. How can you be a virtuous wife, if you are not cloaked in His Word? Yes, you are able to read the bible without being in church and having a church home, but God did not intend for you to walk this spiritual journey alone and without support or accountability. Additionally, belonging to a church and attending regularly gives you the opportunity to glorify God with the gifts He blessed you with. Why is this important? A Kingdom Man (the kind you should want to be married to) will be walking in purpose and striving to glorify God with His gifts in his local congregation. Please know that he will be looking for a woman who is doing the same. Why would he want less? He's looking for a woman who is equally yoked with him in the area of commitment. Moreover, the bible says *not to forsake the assembling of ourselves together (*Hebrews 10:25). This means, as believers we ought to go to church. As a woman who desires God's best, you must be in alignment with God's will first! *Hey, you never know! You may meet your future husband there! If you go to church regularly now, he may even have his eye on you, observing your life, deciding whether he wants to make you his wife!*

Prohibitor #4: Engaging in premarital sex

"The greater the number of sexual partners, the greater the harmful residue, and the greater the long term impact." –Barbara Wilson

"With every additional partner, you decrease your ability to bond...as you increase in marital partners, you decrease in marital satisfaction. –Barbara Wilson

These two quotes say it all! I encourage you to recommit to purity! You *can* do it! Premarital sex does more harm than good. Saved sex is the best sex! When I say "saved" I mean, saving sex for marriage. I encourage you to do this. I believe you want to experience complete marital satisfaction. If so, make a decision to crucify your flesh so you can experience more marital fulfillment in the future.

Prohibitor #5: Maintaining a carnal mindset about love and marriage

Shows like *Basketball Wives*, *Braxton Family Values*, *Scandal*, and *Young & the Restless* will not prepare your mindset for marriage as they give a fictional depiction of what it takes to maintain a God-honoring marriage. In order to prepare mentally and spiritually for marriage I suggest you study bible scriptures which specifically addresses love and marriage like 1 Corinthians 13; The book of Song of Solomon, Ephesians 5, 1 Corinthians 7, Hebrews 13, Genesis 2, and Colossians 3. If you do not rid yourself of a carnal mindset about love and marriage, you will think marriage is about self-satisfaction and sex. You may even believe that it is acceptable for a woman to lead the family when a man is present in the household. You may also be deceived into thinking that boundaries are unnecessary in a marriage, and more! Having a carnal idea of love will cause you to overlook the authentic and pure love that a man of God would lavish upon you. Then you will not be able to recognize a good man even when he is right in front of your face! Sis, get to know what TRUE love is! God and His Word are excellent examples!

Prohibitor #6: Having no vision.
Lack of commitment to personal goals and God's purpose for your life

The relationship with your future husband is not designed to complete you. Your aim should be to become whole and experience fulfillment even without a husband. God would not send you a husband to complete you, your husband is meant to complement.
While you are single, establish your own life and pursue your own dreams. Aim for completeness and satisfaction in your life.

Prohibitor #7: Carrying hurt and offense from your past

It is very simple. You cannot move forward in love and relationships while carrying emotional baggage. Please know that your future marriage is not designed to mirror a counseling relationship nor a recovery center. As I've mentioned in chapter one, go to God so he can heal you completely! It is important that you take this time now in this season of your life to be introspective and real with yourself and with God. Yes, you can enjoy your singleness - and you should, but this is not the time to be in serial relationships. I can tell you from personal experience that hopping in relationships one after the other will not bring you true healing. Sure, a man may bring you happiness, but not healing. In the words of Relationship Coach Tony Gaskins, "*heal before you deal*". Heal before you deal with another relationship. This is the only way you will have the capacity to give and receive true love.

Prohibitor #8: Pursuing and/or persuading a man

Pursuing a man is not what you want to do. Persuading and pursuing a man is actually quite unattractive. Allow a man to be a man. You will experience much more fulfillment in your relationship and marriage when the man has pursued you. When a man pursues, it means that he sees value in you and he wants you! If you have to chase and persuade him, like the movie title, I must tell you the truth, *he's just not that into you!* Ladies lay low. We are not supposed to go out and search for a man. Remember the bible says, *He that FINDS a wife, finds a good thing.* The key word is "he" and "find". You see, that's his job to pursue. When you take on this role, you are literally not positioning yourself to be found, *and* you are not preparing yourself for marriage. Instead, you are preparing yourself to fulfill your own fantasy and false hope. A *real* man wants to lead and pursue. His pursuit of you is his first demonstration of his leadership. I implore you, position yourself to be found; let him pursue you!

Prohibitor #9: Disobedience to God & His Word- Lack of commitment to biblical teaching

As you desire to be married, it is imperative that you are obedient to God's Word. Truth is, even if you do not desire marriage, as a follower of Christ, your lifestyle and decision making should be in alignment to God's Word. Particularly as it relates to your preparation and positioning, you are going to need to *hear* from God. You will want Him to speak to you and give you wisdom as you date and discern if the man you are with is "The One". It is very difficult to be spiritually unified and in-tune with God when you are disobedient. Disobedient simply means that you are not upholding His principles, you are in a lifestyle of sin, you are not following His Word, nor are you allowing Him to be Lord over your life. Sin creates distance between you and God. How can you expect God to bless you with His best, when you are not doing your best to glorify Him with your life? God is not a "tit-for-tat" kind of God, He is merciful and gracious, but the bible says *He is a rewarder of them who diligently seek Him.* This is in regard to prayer, but it also lets us know that when we seek after His righteousness and we are obedient to His Word, we will be rewarded. Don't you want to receive the gift of a husband? *Yes, right!* I encourage you to truly and sincerely live for God! He desires to have a close relationship with you. He desires to bless you; but God will not force you to do anything. Get close to Him. Build your relationship with Him. Walk in obedience and in accordance to His Word. Grow into a spiritually mature and intimate relationship with God. This will *truly* prepare you to be a wife!

Prohibitor #10: Being unwilling to reflect and Acknowledge that you are in need of change/ improvement/renewal.

I pray that out of the many jewels and tips I have shared with you in the book, that you really understand the importance of reflection and being honest with yourself. The only way this book is transformational, as I know God has shared with me that it would be, is if you acknowledge there are some ways, habits, thought patterns, etc. that must change. I believe that a renewed mind and changed life makes a ready wife. If, after you finish reading this book, you put it down and do not feel the need to change a single thing in your life so that you can become a better woman, then just maybe you *aren't* truly serious about positioning and preparing yourself for marriage. Strive to be a better woman now, so you can be the best wife ever! Your future husband is looking for a "good thing"! Don't you want to be her? If so, in this season, take the necessary steps to work on you, so you can be the wife you desire to be in the future!

Ready4TheRing Plan Of Action?

Get out of your own way! Don't prohibit your own preparation and positioning!

That's all! No more action steps to give! I want you to develop your own. I believe you *know* what you need to do.

NOTES:

Chapter 12: Recognizing True Love

❖ *Jewel of Wisdom:*

"Love is more than a feeling. Love is service, sacrifice, selflessness, and more. Love is a choice. Love is an action. It is not until you gain the right perspective of love, that you possess the ability to recognize or express love in its truest form. #Ready4TheRing

Oh, how we *long* for love! I do not know about you, but as a single woman I desired to be loved by a man. Yes, my father loved me - but I wanted that *romantic* love. The love where you stay up all night with your boyfriend talking on the phone until you fall asleep. I wanted the love that gives you butterflies each time you see him. I longed for the day a man would look me in the eyes and say, "I love you" in spite of my flaws, my mistakes, and my insecurities. I believed this love would bring me much joy, fulfillment, and happiness. This kind of love would surely lead me down the aisle as a wife so that I could live *happily-ever-after* with my husband, the *love of my life!*

This type of love certainly sounds good, looks good, and even *feels* good, but until I married my husband, I did not realize that love is MUCH greater! It is perfectly alright for you to desire such love experiences, but I need you to understand that this is just a shallow version of TRUE love, and often times we are deceived into believing that the description above is love in its entirety. Many women have been programmed to believe that as long as you get butterflies in your body, he brings you happiness and joy, and he accepts you just as you are, then honey - you're in L-O-V-E.

This is a myth and a mindset of yours that must change. With this perception of love, you are actually limiting your love experience. If this is all you want and all you need in order to believe you have acquired true love - I must tell you, you *really* haven't loved or experienced it yet completely!

Yes, love "feels" good, but the truth is, it may not always *feel* this way. This love may bring you happiness, but there may be a time when loving another person is tough! Love is more than a feeling. Remember, feelings are fickle, meaning your emotions and feelings fluctuate and change frequently. If love was strictly a feeling, it would be unstable and inconsistent. Who would want a love like that?

TYPES OF LOVE

As I'm sure you have heard before, God is Love. God is the best example of love. Without Him, we would not even know what true love is. I want to share with you biblical principles about love. Knowing them will help you discern whether a man's demonstration of the self-proclaimed love he has for you is authentic or not. These principles will also help you understand how to demonstrate or express your love toward another person.

First, let me start by saying this: There are different types of love described in the bible. Four have been generally defined as *Eros, Philos, Agape, and Storge.* The first three are generally mentioned the most by bible scholars and bible resources.

Eros: Eros is a sensual or erotic longing and love that takes place between a husband and wife. It is acceptable within the confines of a marriage and not designed to be expressed outside of the context of a marital relationship.

Philos or Philia: This is a "brotherly" love; a companionship expression of love. This is the type of love Christians are to practice among each other.

Agape: Agape love represents the divine love God expressed through His son Jesus Christ, and to the world when He have His son to die for us! This love does not come natural to us as humans, but we are to strive to be like Christ daily. This love is selfless and sacrificial.

Storge: This is a love one has for family; vital to the proper functioning of families.

It is important for you to understand the different types of love because in our culture we use the word "love" very loosely! It is no wonder many women are often heartbroken and confused when they believe a man "loves" them. Though men don't typically define the type of love they have toward you when they say the three words "I love you", it is likely he does not mean what you think! With men being such sexual creatures, if the two of you are currently having sex or have in the past, he may say, "I love you" simply because of the sensual longing and attraction he has for you. You then receive his words to mean that he loves you with an agape & storge love and so you are thinking this man is your husband! *Is this shedding some light on your current or past experiences?* It did for me!

Above all, no matter the type of love, there are characteristics of love that Christ has displayed and shared in His Word that ought to be present in any love relationship. On the other hand, His Word also addresses what love is not. So the next time a man says he loves you, or you think you love him - think on the following things.

TRUE LOVE DEFINED

Love is not simply feelings, emotions, admiration, and attraction - but love is ACTION. Love is a verb. Love must be demonstrated. There is a whole chapter in the bible about love which is found in 1 Corinthians chapter 13. Let's focus on versus 4-7. I encourage you to read the whole chapter at a later time. Versus 4-7 are below:

"Love is ***patient****, love is* ***kind****. It does* ***not envy****, it does* ***not boast****, it is* ***not proud****. 5 It does* ***not dishonor*** *others, it is* ***not self-seeking****, it is* ***not easily angered****, it* ***keeps no record of wrongs****. 6 Love does* ***not delight in evil*** *but* ***rejoices with the truth****. 7 It always* ***protects****, always* ***trusts****, always* ***hopes****, always* ***perseveres****."*

Wow! How about that for love! Interestingly, these verses tell us more about what love is not, than what love is. However, the adjectives that describe love are very strong! I have provided further definition of each word in bold font from the scripture to give you an even better understanding of all that love encompasses.

Love is **patient:** It understands; is enduring; it does not rush.

Love is **kind:** It is considerate, generous, friendly.

It **does not envy:** It is not resentful; it does not desire another's possessions. Instead, love celebrates. Love is content.

It **does not boast:** It does not speak with excessive pride. Instead, love is humble and meek.

It is **not proud:** It is not excessive in self-esteem or dignity. Instead, love is respectful and submissive.

It **does not dishonor** others**:** It does not bring shame or disgrace upon another. Instead, love is honoring and noble.

It is **not self-seeking:** It is not selfish. Instead, love is self-less and puts other's needs before your own.

It is **not easily angered:** It is not hostile and aggressive. Instead, love is pleasant, enjoyable, and pleasing.

It **keeps no record of wrongs:** It does not hold grudges, bitterness, or resentment. Instead, love forgives.

Love **does not delight in evil** but **rejoices with the truth:** It is not associated with wrongdoing and sin. It celebrates truth.

It always **protects,** always **trusts,** always **hopes,** always **perseveres:** It remains constant and consistent. It guards from harm, it encompasses faith, and never gives up.

Do you see how love is more than a feeling? When you think back to the men who have told you they loved you, was their love toward you expressed like this? *Probably not.* You are not alone. As I reflected over my relationships, I realized that what was expressed as love was truly lust or a lie. It was not a pure or authentic love at all. I did not even have to go very far in the scripture before this became evident! Verse 4 says "Love is patient", which means it is understanding, tolerant, and it endures. The men I dated were not understanding of my aim to remain pure and wait until marriage to have sex. Nor did they want to endure with me. Maybe they did for a few months, but not much longer after that. Why did I believe that was love? Why have *you* believed this is love? It clearly was not. Sis, I encourage you to no longer simply desire a *love feeling,* but measure a man's self-proclaimed love for you with the Word of God.

The Word says love does not dishonor others. If he is putting you down, using negative slurs, if he is disrespectful in any way - this is not true love. The Word makes it clear that love is not self-seeking. Is he selfish? Does he try to control you? Better yet, are *you* selfish? Must you always have your way or else you will throw a fit or manipulate him to get your way? Let me tell you, *that* is not true love. Love keeps no records of wrong. Does he or do you hold grudges? Do you refuse to see him when you are mad? Do you go and tell all your friends when he makes you upset or do you blast him on Facebook? This is not "love" my dear. Love is kind. These actions are not kind. Whewww! Are you getting the revelation now? Love is expressed through ACTION. If a person's actions are not in alignment with what God's word says about love, then the truth is, they are not demonstrating true love. This goes for your ex, your future man, and even you!

MORE ABOUT TRUE LOVE

Love is sacrificial and love is service. Again, in our society, many people in general view love as something that makes "them" feel good. Love seems to be about *me, me, me.* As women, we want to be in love because we want all that a man can give *us.* I truly need you to know that love is not about you and what you can get. You must know and understand this before you are married. Entering into a marital covenant with that ideal will cause you to be unpleasantly surprised. Remember, love is not self-seeking. Love is about others. Love requires sacrifice. Love requires service and giving unto another. It is not about you.

Think about it, the bible says in John 3:16 "*For God so loved the world that he gave his one and only Son, that whoever believes in him shall not perish but have eternal life.*" God LOVED the world so much that He GAVE His only Son. This is mind-blowing! God gave His *only* son so that WE may have eternal life. This proves that love is a demonstration of selflessness, service, and sacrifice. If love was about self, then God would have kept His only Son and left us to be condemned to hell instead of giving us the opportunity to gain eternal life with Him in Heaven.

So you want to be married? You have to realize what true love is. Are you ready to sacrifice? Sacrifice means to give up, to surrender, to forfeit. Marriage requires sacrifice, and this is a part of love. Are you ready to sacrifice the time you spend with your girlfriends in order to dedicate quality time to your future spouse and marriage relationship? Let me remind you that you will actually need to start doing this before you even get married. While engaged, the two of you need to get to know each other quite well before the marital commitment.

Are you willing to sacrifice your "need to be right" all the time, and to get the last word? Are you ready to serve? As a married woman, you will both serve your husband and you will serve alongside him. When I say serve, I mean give unto a greater cause. This does not mean to be at his beckon call like a peasant. Are you willing to help lighten your spouse's load to make their life a little easier? It's more than cooking dinner. It's helping with household chores, extending your support and kind words, assisting with a project, and yes, striving to meet your husband's sexual & physical needs. It's speaking his "love language" and more! You must remember God uses marriage to mature, develop, and make us more like Him. Christ operated in servant-hood, and so should we!

A HUSBAND'S LOVE

Everything I mentioned above regarding love applies to you and also to your future husband. He is commanded to love you like Christ loves the church. As you desire to be married, as I mentioned in a previous chapter, many distractions and counterfeits will come your way. The only way you will be able to discern the true man of God sent by God is through prayer and using the Word to determine if the man's "love" toward you is in alignment with what God says. Because your marital relationships do not start as such, but moves through different levels such as friendship, dating, engagement, etc. it is vital that you be intentional in examining a man's actions and expressions toward you early on. You cannot allow your feelings to guide you and take the lead. You must be in control of your emotions, be sober, alert, and intentional when dealing with men, while allowing God to speak to you. Love is more than just a feeling!

Meditate and reflect on 1 Corinthians 13:4-7 and remember Christ's example of love which is sacrificial, serving (giving), and selfless. The bible shares much more on love; however, I want to bring one passage of scripture to your attention:

Ephesians 5: 25-33:

[25] Husbands, love your wives, just as Christ loved the church and gave himself up for her [26] to make her holy, cleansing her by the washing with water through the word,[27] and to present her to himself as a radiant church, without stain or wrinkle or any other blemish, but holy and blameless. [28] In this same way, husbands ought to love their wives as their own bodies. He who loves his wife loves himself. [29] After all, no one ever hated their own body, but they feed and care for their body, just as Christ does the church— [30] for we are members of his body. [31] "For this reason a man will leave his father and mother and be united to his wife, and the two will become one flesh." [32] This is a profound mystery—but I am talking about Christ and the church. [33] However, each one of you also must love his wife as he loves himself, and the wife must respect her husband.

In this passage, we see it repeated several times that a husband is called to love his wife as Christ loves the church *and* as he loves himself. Your future husband is expected to love you as Christ does. This is more reason why you should take time to research the bible to gain insight on how Christ demonstrates His love toward His children. Your future husband sure has some "big shoes" to fill, doesn't he?

Remember, marriage is no play thing! Marriage is a life-long commitment, one that is designed to be God-honoring. This is why you cannot allow your decision of who you are going to marry be strictly based on your emotions and the feeling of being loved. No, you must be able to have experienced a man's demonstration of TRUE love *and* YOU must be ready to commit to expressing TRUE love unto him.

THE "S" WORD...NO, IT'S NOT SEX

So the man has the responsibility of loving you as Christ loves the church and you love him back, right? Correct, but there is more to it. Your expression of love encompasses a trait that many women despise, but I have come to love, SUBMISSION.

Here is what the Word of God says:

Ephesians 5:22-24

Wives, submit yourselves to your own husbands as you do to the Lord. [23] *For the husband is the head of the wife as Christ is the head of the church, his body, of which he is the Savior.* [24] *Now as the church submits to Christ, so also wives should submit to their husbands in everything.*

I have heard many women say, "I don't need to listen to him", "He's not the boss of me", "I'm grown, I have a father, and he's not it", "I don't need a man to tell me what I can and cannot do" and more! Well guess what? These same women are either single and have not been "found" by their husband (because they've been found with a bad 'tude') *or* they are no longer married.

The women who do not want to submit are the same women who remain single or have discontented husbands!

With this type of attitude and perspective, what man would want to be bothered with you? With this outlook, why would you think you deserve the blessings of God when your thought process is not in alignment with God's Word?

Again, let me clear the air. Submission is not oppression. Submission does not mean you do not have freedom of choice or expression. Submission does not equate slavery or dominance.

The prefix "Sub" means "under".

The definition of "mission" is a task or job someone is given to do; it is an assignment; a plan, etc.

Essentially, biblical **submission** means to “come up under the mission/assignment/plan that God has given your future husband, and that he has for the household.

When you say “I Do” at the altar, you are saying to Him “I Do” love you, and “I will” submit to you as Christ commands. Future wife, God says to submit to your husband, I’m not making this up. The only way to experience a fulfilling love and marriage relationship is to abide by God’s Word. When you submit to your future husband, it means you are allowing Him to lead. You are supporting and following the mission given to him by God. Just like you submit to God, the bible says you are to submit your husband. When we submit to God, we may not understand all that He is doing, and we may not even agree, because we want to do our own thing, our way - but ultimately when we submit to God’s will for our lives, we benefit and things work in our favor. The same principle will apply in your future marriage. Your submission will have a reward.

If you have unease with the principle of submission and if you despise the idea of submitting to your future husband, I challenge you to reflect on your ability to submit to God completely right now. It is likely you will find that you do not effectively submit to Christ in your life. Until you do this, submission and the ideal of it will not be appealing to you, nor will you have the ability to effectively submit to your husband. If this is you - it is time to mature in your relationship with

Christ. Learn how to submit to God, so you will know how to submit to your husband. That will be one of the ways you demonstrate your true love to him.

THE FOUNDATION OF LOVE

In both passages of scripture found in Ephesians, the husband and wife must love and submit unto each other like unto Christ. This implies that unless a man and woman render love and submission to God first, they will be unable to do the same unto their spouse.

A man cannot love you like Christ loves the church if He does not know *how Christ loves the church.* Your future husband must have a relationship with Christ. He must be His disciple, a follower of Him, and it is imperative that he has an intimate relationship with Christ. Likewise, you cannot submit to your husband, if you do not even submit to Christ. Sis, you must have a strong, intimate relationship with the Lord before you are married.

Do you think it's easy to follow everything that was mentioned in 1 Corinthians 13 when it says love is patient, kind, keeps no records of wrong, doesn't envy, is not easily angered and more? Girl, take it from a married woman. NO, it is not easy all the time. Expressing love in alignment with this scripture is not always fun, it does not always feel good, and it can be hard. It is difficult at times because demonstrating love in these ways is not always my natural response or instinct. Sometimes I want to be mad and hold a grudge with my husband. Sometimes I do not want to submit. Other times I think he does not deserve my forgiveness, and when I have a- million-and-one things to do, I lack a lot ofpatience.

This is why I say love is not a feeling. There are plenty of days when I am just not “feeling it”. BUT- I make a choice to LOVE daily. When I stood at the altar and said “I Do”, I was making a decision to love Julian all the days of my life. Because I have an intimate relationship with the Lord Jesus Christ, I look to Him as my example and my strength to love like He has called me to! Am I perfect? No. Do I fall short sometimes? Yes. But when I do, God speaks to me in His still small voice, and reminds me of His love toward me. He reminds me of how He forgives me daily. His Word reminds me that I need to be patient, kind, submissive, and selfless. God is gracious and He gives me opportunity to love my husband like the wife He designed me to be! I am so grateful for that!

In summary, recognizing true love and expressing true Love is only possible when knowing Christ. Your future husband will not be able to love or lead you, if he does not have an intimate relationship with Christ. You will not be able to love your husband as you should, without Christ.

How can you emulate someone you do not follow?

As you position and prepare yourself for marriage, be positioned at the feet of God. Spend time with Him. Read His Word. Know what He says about marriage and being a wife. Allow God to prepare you by transforming your mind and renewing your heart, so that you can be your husband's "good thing".

"Love is more than a feeling. Love is service, sacrifice, selflessness, and more. Love is a choice. Love is an action. It is not until you gain the right perspective of love, that you possess the ability to recognize and express love in its truest form." #Ready4TheRing

Ready4TheRing Action Plan:
Know True Love by Knowing Christ and His Word

- Explore and research the bible; specifically for love relationships and how Christ demonstrates love. Start by re-reading these verses: 1Corinthians 13: 4-7; Ephesians 5:22-24, Ephesians 5:25-33, and John 3:16.
- Using 1Corinthians 13:4-7 as a guide, write down the characteristics of love which come natural for you, and the areas in which you need to improve.

- ❖ Pray and ask God to strengthen and prepare you to demonstrate love according to 1Corinthians 13:4-7.

- ❖ Pray and ask God to renew your mind; align your perspective of love, as it relates to marriage, to match God's perspective of love.
  Make a commitment to submit your will and life to Him. Ask God to help you submit to your own husband in His perfect timing.

- ❖ Commit to growing closer to God in this season before you are married so that you will have a strong foundation for your marital relationship. You can read your bible and/or devote time to reading on a bible application. Get a devotional book to study characters or stories in the bible. Pray to God and sing songs unto Him in your private time. Make yourself available to Him so He can mold, shape, and mature you into an even better woman so you can be your husband's "good thing".

NOTES:

Chapter 13: Trusting God: Faith Over Feelings

❖ *Jewel of Wisdom:*

"Having faith in God goes beyond what you see and how you feel. Trust God. He is in control and His timing is always perfect!" #Ready4TheRing

So at this point you may be feeling one of two ways,

1.) Well prepared, positioned, and ready to be a wife OR
2.) Ready to truly transform yourself before becoming a wife

I WANT MY MAN, AND I WANT HIM NOW

If #1 suits you, you "believe" you are ready for marriage right now. Your heart may be telling you that you are ready for love. You may think that you should be "found" sometime soon, and within the next few months you believe God should send you your husband.

In response to these emotions, the bible says that your heart is deceitful above all (Jeremiah 17:9), and your thoughts are unreliable. The truth is, your feelings, heart, and thoughts are all influenced by your environment, desires, and your human nature. On the contrary, God is not influenced by anything. He knows the plans He has for you. God is stable and He does not change. God is all-knowing. He is sovereign and His ways are not your ways, neither are His thoughts your thoughts.

This book was written as a guide and as a tool for you as you desire to be married. The information presented was designed to transform your way of thinking and decision making. While reading this book, I trust that God has opened your spiritual eyes to concepts and perceptions that you were once blind to. The plan of action steps were written to help you continue to renew your mind, and transform your life so you can be the best wife in the future.

While you may believe God should send your husband right now, understand that this book was not written as a "get married quick" scheme. This book was written as a seed to help you prepare mentally, emotionally, and spiritually, so when you receive the answer to your prayers (a husband), in God's timing, you are able to stand as a virtuous wife and "good thing" to your husband.

No matter how you "feel" throughout this season, I encourage you to trust that God knows who & what you need when you need it. God will send your husband to find you at His perfect time. Your husband *may* find you in a couple of months, or within a couple of years. Whatever the case may be, you must keep the faith!

If you ever feel down, worried, or impatient, know that I am praying that you keep your FAITH in God. God has not forsaken and forgotten about you. God is with you! God wants to bless you! God has a plan for your life and it is beyond what you can even think or imagine! Trust Him!

A CHANGE HAS COME OVER ME

If #2 best describes you and you believe there is a transformation that must continue to take place in your life after reading this book, no worries! That's actually great! I wrote this book to coach you along the way! Everything I shared with you, are all actions I had to take to be a woman and wife. Some of the mindsets and lifestyle shifts did not take place for me until after I was married, and it caused rough patches in my marriage. I wrote this book just for you! My goal was to help you transform your life prior to making the marital commitment. Sis, it's actually better that you realize this now, before you are married. If not, you would have carried so much baggage and many unhealthy mindsets & habits into your marriage. You are in a much better spot right now! That is why the subtitle of the book is "How To Prepare Yourself for Marriage RIGHT NOW".

TRUSTING GOD: PURPOSE IN EVERY SEASON

Whether you believe you are more prepared now than you were prior to reading this book, or if you are ready to dive into your metamorphosis, I want you to remember that there is purpose attached to every season. The season you are in right now whether you are single, dating, in a committed relationship, or engaged, it has purpose. Your assignment in this season is to seek God about what His plan is and then get in alignment with what He wants you to do. He has great things in store for you! Right now, God may be calling you into a deeper and more intimate relationship with Him. He may be expanding your territory and influence and now is the time for you to launch your business, write your book, or start a new ministry. In this season, God may be calling you to trust Him more so He can show Himself strong and faithful in your life.

God may be shaping, molding, and maturing you in the spiritual disciplines of prayer and praise. I just encourage you to draw closer to God, seek Him, quiet your spirit, and settle you personal desires so His desires can become yours. When you do this, you position yourself to fulfill His plan in this season of your life. Overall, this is a season of preparation and positioning in both your relationship with God and for your relationship with your future husband. That's exciting!

Be reminded that God's Word says that all things work together for the good of them who love Him and are called according to His purpose! God is working inyour favor! Continue to trust Him!

The bible shares with us the principle that when you are faithful over a few things, God will give you more (Matthew 25:23). It is essential that you are a good steward over all God is calling for you to do now both in the natural and in the spirit as it relates to your spiritual relationship with God. Show yourself faithful over a few, and God will bless you with more. Marriage is more! Marriage brings more! Although marriage is more responsibility, it is fun, exciting, and fulfilling! While you are in this season of your life and trusting God to expand your life through marriage, just be sure to enjoy and appreciate the season you are in. There are great things happening to you and for you RIGHT NOW!

Lastly my sister, have FAITH in God over your FEELINGS. Trust Him, because He will direct your path and bring all things into fruition in His perfect timing!

Ready4TheRing Plan Of Action:
Trust God. Prepare For Your Future and Walk In Purpose Now!

- Enjoy your life! Enjoy this season! Experience fulfillment by walking in your purpose. Spend time with God in prayer and devotions. Ask Him to reveal to you your purpose in this season of your life.

- Commit to giving God your all. He wants to have a close relationship with you, He even calls you friend! Allow Him to continue to make you over from the inside out, so you can be an amazing wife to your husband.

- Revisit the chapters in the book that resonated with you the most. Commit to completing the action steps listed and journal your change. You will see later how God has been faithful in growing and keeping you! You'll be *amazed* at how much you've changed by the time you get married!

- Keep these scriptures handy! Commit them to memory. They will keep you encouraged as God continues to prepare and position you to receive the man He is preparing just for you!

Encouraging Scriptures:
Psalm 37:4
Proverbs 3:5-6
Jeremiah 29:11
Romans 8:28
Philippians 4:6-7
Isaiah 40:31
Psalm 107:1
Psalm 100:5

CONCLUSION

Congratulations! You've made it! You have read through the book! My prayer is that the content shared in this book has totally transformed your way of thinking, dating, loving, and living! It is your emotional, mental, and spiritual renewal that prepares you to be in proper physical position to be found! Trust and know that God will send your husband in His perfect timing!

I would love to hear from you! I encourage you to share your stories of how this book has impacted, prepared, challenged, and transformed you! I invite you to post a review and recommendation on Amazon.com and send an email to Info@teresareneehunt.com.

May God Continue to Bless Your Preparation Journey,

Teresa Renee

www.teresareneehunt.com
Facebook: @Ready 4 The Ring with Teresa R. Hunt
Twitter: @teresareneehunt
Instagram: @Ready4TheRing
LinkedIn: @ Teresa Renee Hunt

REFERENCES

[1]CNN. (2009). Comedian Steve Harvey: Women standards too low.
http://www.cnn.com/2009/LIVING/personal/03/23/o.steve.harvey.love.advice/index.html?iref=24hours

[2]Huff Post. (2013). Facebook, divorce linked in new study.
http://www.huffingtonpost.com/2013/06/06facebook-divorce-linked-i_n_3399727.html

[3]Relevant Magazine. (2011). The secret sexual revolution.
http://www.relevantmagazine.com/life/relationship/features/28337-the-secret-sexual-revolution

[4]Wilson, B. (2010). The invisible bond: How to break free from your sexual past. Colorado Spring, CO: Multnomah Books.

ACKNOWLEDGMENTS

Thank you Lord for totally transforming my life and renewing my heart and mind! I thank you for saving my soul and extending your grace and mercy toward me. I honor and acknowledge You because You are so amazing and without You I am nothing!

To my husband, Julian, the love of my life - if it wasn't for God sending you, I would not have even been able to write this book! I am so glad that you "found" me! I am blessed to have you as my husband and I am grateful to God for you! While I was writing this book, your constant words of encouragement when I got weary or concerned during the process, always kept me going. Thank you for praying with me, for me, and even for the lives of the women who would read this book. Lastly, I thank you for loving me completely with my flaws and all. I am so glad to be on this journey of life and purpose with you!

To my awesome, loving, and supporting parents - I love you! Mom, Victoria Scott and Dad, Tyrone Scott. I thank you for praying for me even when I didn't know you were, but I believe it was your prayers that kept me. Thank you for many wonderful family experiences and memories! Know that I am so appreciative of your every sacrifice and for raising me in a home that serves the Lord so I would one day accept Him as my personal Savior and experience His life-changing power! I thank God for blessing me with the best parents ever!

I want to acknowledge more family! To my mom and dad in-love, Pastor James and Dr. Sheila Johnson-Hunt, I am blessed to have you as family and pastors. I am grateful for your love, prayers, leadership, and support! To my beautiful Nan, Elizabeth Hill, I love you and thank you for always supporting me and loving me! To my family: the Scotts, Robinsons, Hunts, Gaines, my Edinboro family, and all my extended family & friends, I am forever grateful for you always believing in me and supporting me! You have always been there to extend your love! I appreciate you!

To the leaders and ministers of the gospel who have spoken over my life: To my father-in-ministry, Pastor Victor J. Grigsby, of my home church Central Baptist in Pittsburgh, PA, thank you for teaching and instilling in me God's Word so I could have a strong foundation in Christ. Pastor Henry Thrower and First Lady Cynthia Thrower, thank you for molding me and shaping me into a woman aligned with God's assignment through prophetic word and spiritual impartation. Your prayers, divine anointing, and spiritual wisdom have kept me walking in my purpose! Thank you Deacon (Aunt) Josephine Robinson, Prophetess (cousin) Beth Ann Crawford, and Messenger Annette Carswell for declaring God's blessing and prophesying over my life regarding my calling and career! To my Central Baptist Church and First Baptist Church families- I thank God for you!

Thank you Dr. LaShonda Fuller, president of Truth UnTold (TUT) Enterprises, LLC for bringing out the best literary skills within me. I am grateful for your gift of patience, expertise with language, and your professional editing services, which helped make this book a success!

As I close, I must give a huge distant hug and acknowledgement to you! Yes, YOU! I am so humbled that you have taken time to read this book and I appreciate you! I thank God for you and I pray that as God has been speaking to you through the pages of this book, that you will develop a more intimate relationship with Him, be obedient, desire to please Him in all that you do, follow His leading, and align your decisions with your desire to be a wife. Your husband will greatly appreciate it!

ABOUT THE AUTHOR

TERESA RENEE HUNT is a Life-Makeover Coach, Marriage Preparation Expert, Speaker, and **Founder** of the Renewed Life Academy and the Renewed & Ready4TheRing Movement. She prepares women to experience the life and love they desire through her personal development firm **Truth2RenewHearts Enterprises LLC**, which houses her coaching programs and courses focusing on identity discovery, life-transformation, and marriage preparation for singles, engaged, and newlywed women.

Having overcome the emotional effects of rape, the baggage of low-self esteem, brokenness from failed relationships, guilt, hurt, shame, regret, and more, Teresa Renee is able to relate and speak to the heart of real issues women face, providing hope, restoration, and serving as a catalyst to their renewal and transformation prior to becoming a wife. Teresa strongly believes "a renewed mind and transformed life prepares & positions a woman to be a virtuous wife". Teresa is married to her husband, Dr. Julian E. Hunt, and they reside in Pittsburgh, Pennsylvania.

Teresa Renee is also the **author** of "*Is He The One?: A Guide To Recognizing The Perfect One For You*". You can download a copy of this insightful book on her website.

To **learn more** about Teresa Renee and working with her directly as your coach or as a speaker for your next event, visit her website at **www.teresareneehunt.com**.

Made in the USA
San Bernardino, CA
26 March 2015